MW00886968

COVER: LAVs of the 2d Marine Division move past burning oil wells in Kuwait.

The 2d Marine Division and Its Regiments

by
Danny J. Crawford, Robert V. Aquilina
Ann A. Ferrante, Lena M. Kaljot, and Shelia P. Gramblin
Reference Section, Historical Branch

HISTORY AND MUSEUMS DIVISION
HEADQUARTERS, U.S. MARINE CORPS
WASHINGTON, D.C.
2001

Table of Contents

2d Marine Division 1
2d Marine Division Commanding Generals 10
2d Marine Division Lineage 12
2d Marine Division Honors 14
The 2d Marine Division Patch 15

The 2d Marines 16
Commanding Officers, 2d Marines 24
2d Marines Lineage 27
2d Marines Honors 29

The 6th Marines 30
Commanding Officers, 6th Marines 38
6th Marines Lineage 41
6th Marines Honors 44

The 8th Marines 45
Commanding Officers, 8th Marines 54
8th Marines Lineage 56
8th Marines Honors 59

The 10th Marines 60
Commanding Officers, 10th Marines 68
10th Marines Lineage 70
10th Marines Honors 73

The 2d Marine Division

The 2d Marine Division is the direct descendant of the 2d Marine Brigade, which was activated on 1 July 1936 at San Diego, California. Within a year of its activation, the brigade was called upon to reinforce the 4th Marines in China, when unstable conditions threatened American lives and property in Shanghai's International Settlement. Arriving in Shanghai on 19 September 1937, the brigade occupied defensive positions within the American sector of the international zone. When the immediate threat to American lives had passed, the brigade, less the 4th Marines, was withdrawn and redeployed to California during February-April 1938.

As the prospect of war increased during 1940, the Marine Corps expanded. An immediate reflection of this increase in strength was the creation of division-sized organizations. Accordingly, the 2d Marine Division was officially activated 1 February 1941 at Camp Elliott near San Diego, California, dropping its earlier designation as the 2d Marine Brigade. Major General Clayton B. Vogel became the first commanding general of the division. By

2d Division Marines prepare to advance toward the front lines in trucks captured from Japanese forces in the midst of the intense fighting on Guadalcanal in December 1942.

Department of Defense Photo (USMC) A51400

late spring of 1941, the division consisted of three infantry regiments, the 2d, 6th, and 8th Marines; an artillery regiment, the 10th Marines; service, medical, and engineer battalions; and transport, service, tank, signal, chemical, and antiaircraft machine gun companies.

Each of the three infantry regiments in the new division brought a wealth of Marine Corps combat tradition. The 2d Marines had landed at Veracruz, Mexico, in 1914, and at Haiti in 1915. The 6th Marines had fought in France during World War I, and had seen action in the Dominican Republic and Cuba in 1924. The 8th Marines had manned the Texas border during 1917-1918, and had fought in Haiti during the early 1920s.

As the threat of war intensified, the 6th Marines; the 2d Battalion, 10th Marines; and reinforcing tank, medical, service, and engineering units formed the 1st Provisional Marine Brigade. They sailed for Iceland during May and June 1941 to counter the threat of an anticipated German invasion. The 2d Engineer Battalion was similarly detached and sent to Hawaii in the fall of 1941, where it helped to defend Pearl Harbor during the Japanese attack of 7 December.

Department of Defense Photo (USMC) A62054
LtGen Alexander A. Vandegrift, right, commanding general of all Southwest Pacific Marine forces, confers with MajGen Julian C. Smith, the commanding general of the 2d Marine Division, near Wellington, New Zealand, September 1943.

Marines assault a bomb-proof shelter just off the beach at Tarawa on 20 November 1943.
Department of Defense Photo (USMC) A63930

Immediately after the outbreak of war, the 2d Marine Division, in conjunction with U.S. Army units, was assigned the mission of defending the California coast against possible Japanese invasion. Similarly, the 8th Marines, reinforced by other units from the division, was designated part of a new 2d Marine Brigade, which sailed from San Diego on 6 January 1942 to assume the defense of American Samoa. After the immediate danger of invasion had passed, the division was relieved of its defensive duties, and began the task of reforming into an amphibious assault organization. The 9th Marines became part of the division for a few months. On 1 April 1942, the 6th Marines, back from Iceland, rejoined the division.

By late summer of 1942, the 2d Marine Division was ready to participate in the first United States ground offensive of World War II—the Guadalcanal campaign. In early August 1942 the 2d Marines, along with supporting elements and 1st Marine Division units, landed on Tulagi, Gavutu, and Florida Islands, distinguishing themselves in bitter fighting during the opening days of the Guadalcanal operation. The 8th Marines arrived on Guadalcanal early in November 1942, and the 6th Marines in January 1943. Now fighting for the first time as a full division, the 2d Marine Division, in conjunction with Army units, succeeded in driving the Japanese back to the westernmost part of the island. Combat operations on Guadalcanal included tank-infantry attacks and point-blank artillery fire, along with grenade and small arms assaults. Organized enemy resistance collapsed early in February 1943. By the end of that month, all units of the 2d Marine Division (with the exception of the 3d Battalion, 18th Marines, and the Seabee battalion of the engineer regiment) embarked for New Zealand, to begin eight months of rehabilitation and retraining.

The 2d Marine Division, commanded by Major

A 2d Marine Division patrol, using a demolition charge, flushes out a stubborn Japanese soldier during the rugged fighting on Saipan on 24 June 1944.

Department of Defense Photo (USMC) A83282

Marines from the 2d Division wade ashore on Tinian in late July 1944.

General Julian C. Smith, opened the drive through the Central Pacific with an assault on Betio Island at Tarawa Atoll in the Gilbert Islands, in the early morning hours of 20 November 1943. The ensuing 76 hours at Tarawa saw some of the fiercest fighting in Marine Corps history. Withering defensive fire from Japanese machine guns and mortars inflicted heavy Marine casualties during the landing, making it difficult to secure a toehold. On D+1, the Marines began to move inland. Despite intense resistance, Betio was secured by 23 November. Five days later the entire atoll was in friendly hands. The battle for Tarawa was the first real Navy and Marine Corps test of amphibious assault doctrine and techniques, which would be refined during subsequent operations in the Pacific. At Tarawa, the 2d Marine Division suffered more than 3,000 casualties. In December 1943, the last elements of the division sailed from Tarawa to rejoin the parent unit now located on the island of Hawaii.

On Hawaii, the 2d Marine Division began intensive training to prepare for its next operation. By early May 1944, the division learned that its next mission, in conjunction with the 4th Marine Division and the U.S. Army's 27th Infantry Division, would be the assault and seizure of Saipan and Tinian in the Mariana Islands. The capture of the Marianas was central to allied strategy in the Central Pacific campaign. The islands would provide air and sea bases to bring the war directly to Japan.

On 15 June 1944, assault waves of the 6th and 8th Marines landed on the southwestern beaches of Saipan, against moderate resistance. Japanese mortar fire began to build up, however, as the defenders reacted to the initial landings. The Marines pushed steadily forward against stiffening resistance. The remaining elements of the 2d and 4th Marine Divisions were landed on the following day. Later, the Marines would encounter a system of well-defended caves and a last-ditch Japanese counterattack, but after three weeks of fighting, the island was declared secure on 9 July 1944. The seizure of Saipan led to construction of the first base in the Pacific for B-29 bombing missions against the Japanese home islands.

On 24 July 1944, elements of the 2d Marine Division conducted a successful offshore feint near Tinian Town, while units of the 4th Marine Division landed on the northwest beaches of Tinian. The 2d Marine Division landed on the following day and joined forces with the 4th Marine Division to eliminate Japanese resistance from the southern end of the island. After elements of the 2d Marine Division successfully repulsed Japanese banzai attacks on 1 August, organized resistance on the island ceased. The 2d Marine Division units returned to Saipan to resume mopping-up operations. On 27 March 1945, the division left Saipan to take part in the battle for the Ryukyus.

The landings on Okinawa began on 1 April 1945. The 2d Marine Division was employed as a floating reserve that made feints along the southern approaches to Okinawa. The unopposed main landings were made by Marines and units of the U.S. Tenth Army on the north-central beaches. The 2d Marine Division remained at sea until 11 April, when it returned to Saipan after sending Seabees and amphibian trucks ashore.

In mid-May, during the course of the Ryukyus campaign, the 2d Marine Division had to furnish units to seize two small islands, Iheya and Aguni,
located near Okinawa. A task force composed of the 8th Marines; the 2d Battalion, 10th Marines; and other supporting units, made an unopposed landing on Iheya on 3 June. The island was secured the following day. Aguni was taken on 9 June, again without opposition. The same task force was redeployed several days later to Okinawa. It was placed under the operational control of the 1st Marine Division for the final drive of the Ryukyus campaign. After completing mop-up operations on Okinawa, all 2d Marine Division units were redeployed to Saipan by mid-July 1945.

The end of hostilities in September 1945 did not signal the end of the 2d Marine Division's role in the Pacific. From September 1945 until June 1946, the division took part in the occupation of Japan, primarily on the island of Kyushu. In July 1946, the division finally relocated to Camp Lejeune, North Carolina. At greatly reduced strength, it settled into a peacetime routine.

During the first few postwar years, the division conducted training exercises and maneuvers in the Atlantic and on the East Coast of the United States.

2d Division Marines on a street in Nagasaki on 23 September 1945 during the occupation of Japan.
Department of Defense Photo (USMC) A139774

Department of Defense Photo (USMC) A17500

A 2d Marine Division machine gun crew is positioned on a rooftop in the dock area of Beirut, Lebanon, on 23 July 1958, alert for any contingency that might arise.

In February 1948, the 8th Marines, then at one-battalion strength, sailed for the Mediterranean in response to developing crises in Greece and Turkey. This marked the beginning of a series of forward afloat deployments with the Sixth Fleet that continues to this day. Throughout this period, the 2d Marine Division has provided landing teams and Marine air-ground task forces for service in the Caribbean as well.

The 2d Marine Division's role as a force-in-readiness was tested by the outbreak of war in Korea, in June 1950. Many of the division's personnel were integrated into units of the understrength 1st Marine Division through redesignations and unit transfers to the West Coast, but the 2d Marine Division itself was also brought up quickly to wartime strength. After an intensive training program, it was pronounced ready for any assignment, but did not deploy to Korea.

The division's combat readiness would next be tested during the summer of 1958. On 14 July, three reinforced battalions from the 2d Marine Division, which were then afloat in the Mediterranean with the Sixth Fleet, were ordered into Lebanon. Units of the division were ashore on the beaches of Lebanon within hours of the decision to land, and were joined several days later by air-transported elements of the 2d Battalion, 8th Marines, from Camp Lejeune, North Carolina. Remaining in Lebanon until October, the Marines in and around Beirut helped to maintain political stability, to preserve law and order, and to protect American lives and property. In all, more than 6,000 Marines were committed to the 1958 Lebanon operation, in conjunction with U.S. Army units.

The division's ability to respond decisively in an emergency situation was tested again barely four years later. The Cuban missile crisis of October

Department of Defense Photo (USMC) A19478

Marines of the 2d Division storm ashore in combat gear on Onslow Beach at Camp Lejeune, North Carolina, in an amphibious landing exercise during February 1964.

1962 brought the deployment of most of the 2d Marine Division to Guantanamo Bay and the waters off Cuba. Remaining in the Caribbean until early December, the division had once again demonstrated its ability to respond to short-notice embarkation orders with speed and efficiency.

The chaotic conditions created by a Communist-inspired coup in the Dominican Republic during April 1965 led to American intervention. Marines went ashore and entered the capital city of Santo Domingo to protect the lives of American citizens, and to assist in the evacuation of refugees. Units of the division—in all, four reinforced battalions—helped more than 1,300 evacuees during the six-week mission in the Dominican Republic.

During the 1970s, the 2d Marine Division conducted comprehensive training programs to increase combat efficiency and to maintain the capability of responding rapidly to emergencies. Amphibious exercises, many involving North Atlantic Treaty Organization (NATO) allies, were held routinely throughout the Caribbean, the Atlantic, and the Mediterranean. The division's units received rigorous combined arms training under live fire conditions at the Marine Air-Ground Combat Center at Twentynine Palms, California; cold weather and mountain warfare training in the Sierra Nevadas; and jungle warfare training in Panama, among other opportunities.

The 2d Marine Division's ability to meet the fast breaking challenges of an uncertain world has continued to be tested through an unending series of alerts, evacuations, and other non-routine deployments. From the summer of 1982, through early 1984, division units served on a rotating basis as peacekeeping forces in Lebanon, accepting the hazards inherent in such a mission with courage and professionalism. In October 1983, as well, the division provided the ground combat element for the Marine landing force that took part in a deftly-executed, short-notice intervention in Grenada.

Throughout the remainder of the decade, the

Department of Defense Photo (USN) DN-ST-84-01282

Men of the 2d Marine Division arrive at vacated buildings of the Lebanese Scientific University in February 1983 to take up watch positions in the northern portion of the 22d Marine Amphibious Unit's perimeter around Beirut International Airport.

division and its regiments conducted numerous training operations to maintain a high level of preparedness. From December 1989 to January 1990, elements of the division participated in Operation Just Cause, a joint operation with the U.S. Army, Navy, and Air Force which helped to restore order and democracy in the Central American nation of Panama.

The 2 August 1990 Iraqi invasion of Kuwait threatened the stability of the entire Persian Gulf region. President George H. Bush ordered the deployment of U.S. Armed Forces to the region, to prevent a possible Iraqi invasion of neighboring Saudi Arabia. As the 2d Marine Division prepared to deploy to the Persian Gulf, the Secretary of Defense authorized the Marine Corps to call up 15,000 reservists. Increments of mobilized Reserve units soon began to arrive at Camp Lejeune for processing and integration into the active forces. On 18 November, the 2d Marine Division received the expected orders to deploy to the Kuwait theater of operations.

After an elaborate 10 December review at Camp Lejeune, the main body of the division began its movement to Saudi Arabia. The 2d Marine Division formally established its presence in Saudi Arabia on 14 December 1990, with the arrival of its Commanding General, Major General William M. Keys. Over the next several weeks, units continued to arrive and join the division. The division's main command post arrived in the vicinity of Al Kibrit on 14 January, with other elements arriving as late as the 24th.

The division began immediate training and preparation for mechanized operations and the breaching of Iraqi minefields. On 10 January 1991, the U.S. Army's 1st Brigade, 2d Armored Division (the "Tiger Brigade"), reported to operational control of the 2d Marine Division, and would prove to be of great benefit during the ensuing campaign. With the arrival of this important brigade, the division's assembly in theater was complete.

By the end of January, the division had begun planning for movement to final assembly areas and, on 27 January, conducted its first offensive operation with an artillery raid against Iraqi positions. By 19 February the division had completed its move to Al Khanjar in preparation for the major allied coalition assault into Kuwait and Iraq. At H-Hour on 24 February, division engineers blew lanes across enemy minefields, which cleared the six lanes necessary for the passage of 2d Marine Division units. After breaking through the obstacles, the division fanned out towards Al Jaber Airfield. Enemy opposition was initially light, consisting mostly of intermittent shelling. On 25 and 26 February, Iraqi armored counterattacks hit the right flank of the division, and were defeated with heavy enemy losses.

Through the execution of rapid maneuver and the skillful application of firepower, Iraqi forces were soon overwhelmed. By outflanking the enemy and destroying their heavy equipment with air and artillery fire, the division gave the Iraqis the choice of surrendering or dying where they stood. In the thousands, they chose the former. By 27 February, the division had consolidated its positions outside of Al Jahrah and Al Kuwait, and cleared the last pockets of Iraqi resistance. On 28 February, a ceasefire was ordered.

During the 100 hours of combat in which the 2d Marine Division was engaged, it amassed an impressive amount of enemy equipment and troops: more than 13,000 prisoners taken and 533 tanks, 127 artillery pieces, 291 armored personnel

Department of Defense Photo (USMC) DM-SC-92-01211

An infantryman of the 2d Marine Division mans a fighting hole as part of a drill at the division combat operations center in Saudi Arabia during Operation Desert Storm.

carriers, and 45 pieces of antiaircraft artillery either destroyed or captured. It was truly an impressive achievement. Elements of the division remained in Southwest Asia to participate in Operation Provide Comfort, which provided disaster relief and established security zones for Kurdish refugees in Iraq. The bulk of the division began its redeployment from the Gulf in April, receiving a well-deserved welcome home at Camp Lejeune.

During the immediate post-Desert Storm years, and throughout the remainder of the decade, elements of the 2d Marine Division participated in military operations and humanitarian missions in areas as diverse as Liberia (Operation Sharp Edge), Haiti (Operation Support Democracy), Somalia (Operation Restore Hope), and Cuba (Operation Sea Signal) in support of American interests at home and abroad. These operations provided humanitarian support, non-combatant evacuations, and in the instance of Haiti, helped to restore democracy and rebuild the nation. Closer to home; elements of the division participated during 1993-94 in Operations Able Manner and Able Vigil, which supported the interdiction of Haitian and Cuban migrants in the Florida Straits.

The 2d Marine Division has also supported continued American foreign policy interests in Europe. During the last years of the decade, elements of the division participated in support of NATO operations in Bosnia, and later Albania and Kosovo, as ethnic strife in the former Yugoslavia threatened the stability of Eastern Europe.

A mechanized patrol of Battalion Landing Team 3/8 halts to interact with children in Gnjilane, Kosovo, in July 1999.

Photo courtesy of Maj Nathan S. Lowrey, USMCR

9

2d Marine Division
Commanding Generals

MajGen Clayton B. Vogel .... 1 February 1941 - 7 December 1941
MajGen Charles F. B. Price .... 8 December 1941 - 23 March 1942
BGen Joseph C. Fegan .... 24 March 1942 - 31 March 1942
MajGen John Marston .... 1 April 1942 - 30 April 1943
MajGen Julian C. Smith .... 1 May 1943 - 10 April 1944

MajGen Thomas E. Watson .... 11 April 1944 - 22 June 1945
MajGen Leroy P. Hunt .... 23 June 1945 - 9 July 1946
Col Gregon A. Williams .... 10 July 1946 - 20 July 1946
MajGen Thomas E. Watson .... 21 July 1946 - 31 January 1948
MajGen Franklin A. Hart .... 1 February 1948 - 30 June 1950

MajGen Ray A. Robinson .... 1 July 1950 - 6 December 1951
MajGen Edwin A. Pollock .... 7 December 1951 - 2 September 1952
MajGen Randolph McC. Pate .... 3 September 1952 - 29 May 1953
BGen Robert E. Hogaboom .... 30 May 1953 - 23 June 1953
MajGen George F. Good, Jr. .... 24 June 1953 - 1 July 1954

MajGen Lewis B. Puller .... 2 July 1954 - 7 February 1955
MajGen Edward W. Snedeker .... 8 February 1955 - 1 July 1955
MajGen Reginald H. Ridgeley, Jr. .... 2 July 1955 - 2 June 1957
MajGen Joseph C. Burger .... 3 June 1957 - 24 October 1959
BGen Odell M. Conoley .... 25 October 1959 - 5 November 1959

MajGen James P. Berkeley .... 6 November 1959 - 3 November 1961
MajGen Frederick L. Wieseman .... 4 November 1961 - 23 June 1963
BGen Rathvon McC. Tompkins .... 24 June 1963 - 26 September 1963
MajGen William J. Van Ryzin .... 27 September 1963 - 11 April 1965
MajGen Ormond R. Simpson .... 12 April 1965 - 21 November 1967

MajGen Edwin B. Wheeler .... 22 November 1967 - 18 May 1969
MajGen Michael P. Ryan .... 19 May 1969 - 4 June 1971
BGen Robert D. Bohn .... 5 June 1971 - 28 September 1971
MajGen Fred E. Haynes, Jr. .... 29 September 1971 - 9 January 1973
BGen Arthur J. Poillon .... 10 January 1973 - 1 July 1973

MajGen Samuel Jaskilka .... 2 July 1973 - 19 December 1973
BGen William H. Lanagan, Jr. .... 20 December 1973 - 15 May 1974
MajGen William G. Joslyn .... 16 May 1974 - 30 June 1976
MajGen Kenneth McLennan .... 1 July 1976 - 17 May 1978
MajGen Edward J. Bronars .... 18 May 1978 - 27 June 1979

MajGen David M. Twomey .... 28 June 1979 - 4 June 1981
MajGen Alfred M. Gray, Jr. .... 5 June 1981 - 28 August 1984
MajGen Dennis J. Murphy .... 29 August 1984 - 29 October 1987
MajGen Orlo K. Steele .... 30 October 1987 - 26 September 1989
MajGen William M. Keys .... 27 September 1989 - 24 June 1991

MajGen Paul K. Van Riper . . . . 25 June 1991 - 3 April 1993
MajGen Richard I. Neal . . . . 4 April 1993 - 28 July 1994
MajGen James L. Jones . . . . .29 July 1994 - 23 June 1995
MajGen Lawrence H. Livingston .24 June 1995 - 24 July 1997
MajGen Emil R. Bedard . . . . .25 July 1997 - 29 June 1999

MajGen Robert R. Blackman, Jr. .30 June 1999 -

2d Marine Division
LINEAGE

1936 - 1940

ACTIVATED 1 JULY 1936 AT SAN DIEGO, CALIFORNIA, AS THE
2D MARINE BRIGADE, FLEET MARINE FORCE

DEPLOYED DURING AUGUST-SEPTEMBER 1937 TO SHANGHAI, CHINA

RELOCATED DURING FEBRUARY-APRIL 1938 TO SAN DIEGO, CALIFORNIA

1941 - 1957

REDESIGNATED 1 FEBRUARY 1941 AS THE 2D MARINE DIVISION,
FLEET MARINE FORCE

ELEMENTS DEPLOYED TO ICELAND, JULY 1941 - MARCH 1942

DEPLOYED TO THE SOUTH PACIFIC DURING JANUARY 1942 - JANUARY 1943

PARTICIPATED IN THE FOLLOWING WORLD WAR II CAMPAIGNS

GUADALCANAL
SOUTHERN SOLOMONS
TARAWA
SAIPAN
TINIAN
OKINAWA

DEPLOYED DURING SEPTEMBER 1945 TO NAGASAKI, JAPAN

PARTICIPATED IN THE OCCUPATION OF JAPAN, SEPTEMBER 1945 - JUNE 1946

RELOCATED DURING JUNE-JULY 1946 TO CAMP LEJEUNE, NORTH CAROLINA

1958 - 1988

ELEMENTS PARTICIPATED IN THE LANDINGS IN LEBANON, JULY-NOVEMBER 1958

PARTICIPATED IN THE CUBAN MISSILE CRISIS, OCTOBER-DECEMBER 1962

ELEMENTS PARTICIPATED IN THE INTERVENTION IN THE DOMINICAN REPUBLIC, APRIL-JUNE 1965

PARTICIPATED IN NUMEROUS TRAINING EXERCISES THROUGH THE 1970S

ELEMENTS PARTICIPATED AS PART OF THE MULTINATIONAL PEACEKEEPING FORCE IN LEBANON,
AUGUST 1982 - FEBRUARY 1984

ELEMENTS PARTICIPATED IN THE LANDINGS ON GRENADA - CARRIACOU,
OCTOBER-NOVEMBER 1983

1989 - 1999

ELEMENTS PARTICIPATED IN OPERATION JUST CAUSE, PANAMA,
DECEMBER 1989 - JANUARY 1990

ELEMENTS PARTICIPATED IN OPERATION SHARP EDGE, LIBERIA,
MAY 1990 - JANUARY 1991

PARTICIPATED IN OPERATIONS DESERT SHIELD AND DESERT STORM,
SOUTHWEST ASIA, DECEMBER 1990 - APRIL 1991

ELEMENTS PARTICIPATED IN OPERATION PROVIDE COMFORT, IRAQ, APRIL-JULY 1991

ELEMENTS PARTICIPATED IN OPERATIONS IN SOMALIA, DECEMBER 1992 - MARCH 1994

ELEMENTS PARTICIPATED IN OPERATIONS IN HAITI,
OCTOBER 1993 - OCTOBER 1994

ELEMENTS PARTICIPATED IN HAITIAN REFUGEE OPERATIONS, CUBA,
NOVEMBER 1991 - DECEMBER 1995

ELEMENTS PARTICIPATED IN OPERATIONS ABLE MANNER AND ABLE VIGIL,
FLORIDA STRAITS, JANAURY 1993 - OCTOBER 1994

ELEMENTS PARTICIPATED IN OPERATIONS IN BOSNIA, AUGUST 1994, JUNE 1995 - FEBRUARY 1996

ELEMENTS PARTICIPATED IN OPERATION ASSURED RESPONSE,
LIBERIA, APRIL-AUGUST 1996

ELEMENTS PARTICIPATED IN OPERATIONS IN KOSOVO,
MARCH-JULY 1999

2d Marine Division
HONORS

PRESIDENTIAL UNIT CITATION STREAMER

WORLD WAR II
TARAWA - 1943

NAVY UNIT COMMENDATION STREAMER

SOUTHWEST ASIA
1990 - 1991

MARINE CORPS EXPEDITIONARY STREAMER WITH ONE BRONZE STAR

CHINA SERVICE STREAMER

AMERICAN DEFENSE SERVICE STREAMER WITH ONE BRONZE STAR

EUROPEAN-AFRICAN-MIDDLE EASTERN CAMPAIGN STREAMER

ASIATIC-PACIFIC CAMPAIGN STREAMER WITH ONE SILVER AND TWO BRONZE STARS

WORLD WAR II VICTORY STREAMER

NAVY OCCUPATION SERVICE STREAMER WITH "ASIA" AND "EUROPE"

NATIONAL DEFENSE SERVICE STREAMER WITH TWO BRONZE STARS

ARMED FORCES EXPEDITIONARY STREAMER WITH THREE BRONZE STARS

SOUTHWEST ASIA SERVICE STREAMER WITH THREE BRONZE STARS

THE 2D MARINE DIVISION PATCH

THE 2D MARINE DIVISION SHOULDER PATCH WAS AUTHORIZED FOR WEAR BY UNITS WHICH SERVED WITH OR WERE ATTACHED TO THE DIVISION IN THE PACIFIC DURING WORLD WAR II. DESIGNED AND APPROVED IN LATE 1943, THE INSIGNIA IS IN THE OFFICIAL MARINE CORPS COLORS OF SCARLET AND GOLD. THE INSIGNIA DISPLAYS A SPEARHEAD-SHAPED SCARLET BACKGROUND WITH A HAND HOLD-ING ALOFT A LIGHTED GOLD TORCH. A SCARLET NUMERAL "2" IS SUPERIMPOSED UPON THE TORCH, AND THE TORCH AND HAND IS ENCIRLED BY FIVE WHITE STARS IN THE ARRANGEMENT OF THE SOUTHERN CROSS CONSTELLATION, UNDER WHICH THE DIVISION'S FIRST WORLD WAR II COMBAT TOOK PLACE–AT GUADALCANAL. THE WEARING OF UNIT SHOULDER PATCHES BY MARINES WAS DIS-CONTINUED IN 1947.

The 2d Marines

The 2d Marines was orginally activated on 19 June 1913 as the 1st Advance Base Regiment at Philadelphia, Pennsylvania, under the command of Lieutenant Colonel Charles G. Long. The unit became part of the Advance Base Brigade in December 1913 and was redesignated the 1st Regiment, Advance Base Brigade, on 18 February 1914. The regiment had participated in a number of training maneuvers in Puerto Rico, Florida, and Louisiana when political conditions began to deteriorate in Mexico. Marine Corps forces were ordered to land at Veracruz after President Woodrow

Marines at Veracruz, Mexico, 1914, are, from left: Capt Frederick H. Delano, SgtMaj John H. Quick, LtCol Wendell C. Neville, Col John A. Lejeune, and Maj Smedley D. Butler. Col Neville and Maj Butler of the 2d Marines were both awarded Medals of Honor for their distinguished conduct during the fighting at Veracruz.

Department of Defense Photo (USMC) A302177

16

Wilson received word that a German merchant ship was going there with a cargo of arms. On 22 April 1914, the 1st Regiment landed at Veracruz and joined other forces in clearing the city. Two of the regiment's officers, Major Smedley D. Butler and Lieutenant Colonel Wendell C. Neville, who would later become 14th Commandant of the Marine Corps, received Medals of Honor for distinguished conduct in the battle. The regiment remained there as part of an occupation force for the next seven months, but with the advent of a new and stable government, left Veracruz on 23 November for Philadelphia.

On 3 December 1914, the Advance Base Brigade was reorganized. The 1st Regiment, the fixed defense regiment, was assigned a fire control unit and eight companies, which included four 5-inch gun companies, a searchlight company, a mine company, an engineer company, and an antiaircraft company. The increase of firepower inherent in this reorganization strengthened the regiment's capabilities for the further developments of the Marine Advance Base Force.

By the summer of 1915, internal disorder and revolution in the Republic of Haiti had become critical, jeopardizing American lives and property. On 15 August, the 1st Regiment landed at Cap Haitien, to begin a long period of occupation and "bush" warfare. The regiment carried out extensive patrolling into the interior of the country, in search of Caco bandits. Gunnery Sergeant Daniel J. Daly received his second Medal of Honor for his out-

standing contribution to the success of these operations. The Marines had many encounters with the Haitian rebels. These included the attack and capture of Fort Riviere on 17 November 1915, where Major Butler received his second Medal of Honor. Marines assaulted the old French bastion, located on the summit of Montagne Noir, and overwhelmed the enemy in the fort during a vicious hand-to-hand fray.

After the capture of Fort Riviere and other forts, Haiti became relatively stable. Even as the regiment continued to garrison a number of Haitian towns, some of its rifle companies were sent to the neighboring Dominican Republic. During the early months of 1916, internal disorders there had threatened American lives and property. After order had been restored, the regiment was redesignated as the 2d Regiment, 1st Brigade, on 1 July 1916. Its primary activity then shifted to training of the newly formed Haitian Constabulary, as well as its own Marines.

With the decrease in bandit activity, the 2d Regiment spent the World War I years in routine barracks duty in the tropics. By March 1919, however, rebellions had erupted again in Haiti. The 2d Regiment took to the field, as the native gendarmerie failed to contain the increasing disorder. During May, the regiment mounted a concerted drive to clear the country of bandits. Within a few months, it had mopped up most rebel strongholds.

The next decade in Haiti was relatively peaceful. The 2d Regiment continued to perform duties

Instruction with compasses was part of many routine field training exercises conducted by the 63d Company, 2d Regiment, while stationed in Haiti during January 1926.

that included training and supervising the native constabulary, patrolling and mapping, and quelling political disturbances. On 1 January 1933, as part of a Marine Corps-wide redesignation of units, the 2d Regiment was redesignated as the 2d Marines and assigned to the 1st Brigade. Slightly more than a year later, the 1st Brigade left Haiti, and the 2d Marines was disestablished on 15 August 1934.

The regiment was reactivated 1 February 1941, at San Diego, California, as part of the 2d Marine Division. Under the command of Colonel John M. Arthur, it deployed to Koro Island on 25 July 1942, in time for the final rehearsal for the Guadalcanal landing. Although its mission was one of division reserve, elements of the regiment landed on Florida Island on 7 August 1942, prior to the main assault on Guadalcanal, to support the Tulagi landing. Other elements landed on Gavutu and Tanambogo, to reinforce units engaged in clearing operations. Two infantry battalions of the regiment landed on Tulagi on 9 August and secured the small islands in the area.

On 29 October the 2d Marines moved to Guadalcanal, to take part in the attack towards Kokumbona. Through 11 January 1943, the regiment occupied several defensive positions within the Guadalcanal perimeter, reinforcing the front lines where most needed. It launched a final three-day offensive drive to the west of Point Cruz on 12 January, before reassembling in a reserve area. On 31 January 1943, the regiment left Guadalcanal for New Zealand, arriving in Wellington a few weeks later. Here, for the next nine months, the 2d Marines would rest, train, and reorganize.

The regiment sailed on 28 October 1943, for Efate, south of Espiritu Santo, for final rehearsals of the landing at Tarawa. On 20 November, under the command of Colonel David M. Shoup, the 2d Marines assaulted Betio Island, the defensive bastion of the Japanese force on Tarawa Atoll. The assault waves mounted in amphibian tractors crossed the large coral reef which surrounded the island and moved steadily to shore. The 3d Battalion of the 2d Marines was the first unit to reach its assigned beach and gain a foothold. Later waves embarked in landing craft, had trouble cross-

2d Marines advancing on the city of Garapan during the assault on Saipan in June 1944.

Department of Defense Photo (USMC) A85016

Department of Defense Photo (USMC) A87675

Above, Col David M. Shoup at work on Tinian Island in July 1944. Col Shoup, commanding officer of the 2d Marines during November-December 1943, was awarded a Medal of Honor for his heroic actions during the assault and capture of Tarawa in November. Below, infantrymen of the 2d Marines pause on a street in Nagasaki, Japan, in September 1945.

ing the reef, and were forced to wade hundreds of yards to shore under intense fire. Despite heavy losses, the landing force managed to secure Betio within three days. Colonel Shoup was awarded the Medal of Honor.

On 24 November the 2d Marines left Tarawa for Hawaii, where a new camp awaited it at Kamula. Here at Camp Tarawa, the regiment began the task of rehabilitation, reorganization, and intensive training for battles still ahead. Six months later it left Hawaii for the attack on Saipan. Now under the command of Lieutenant Colonel Walter J. Stuart, the 2d Marines were to feint a diversionary landing on 15 June 1944 in the Tanapag area, then to operate in support of the main landing force. Once ashore, the 2d Marines launched an attack toward Garapan on 17 June. A week later, advancing against stiff enemy opposition, the regiment reached the outskirts of Garapan. Here it remained, patrolling and consolidating its lines, while other elements of the division moved into position for a push northward. On 2 July the regiment began its attack through Garapan, taking the town within two days. From 6 to 11 July, the 2d Marines continued to advance, finally helping to compress the enemy into a small area on the northern tip of

Department of Defense Photo (USMC) A139775

the island. Saipan was declared secure on 9 July, but isolated pockets of resistance kept mop-up operations going until 23 July.

On the following day, the 2d Marines conducted another feint landing, this time off Tinian Town, in support of landing forces to the north. A day later, the regiment landed and advanced rapidly against sporadic enemy resistance to help capture the island. After Tinian was declared secured on 1 August, the regiment once again began the task of mopping up.

After the Tinian operation, the 2d Marines returned to Saipan for rehabilitation and reorganization. The regiment remained there for the next seven months, training under semi-battle conditions, as Japanese stragglers continued to emerge from the jungle long after the fighting was officially over.

The 2d Marines sailed for Okinawa on 25 March 1945, under the command of Colonel Richard M. Cutts, Jr. With other forces the regiment was again executing a diversionary landing when a Japanese kamikaze smashed through one of the landing ships, killing and wounding a number of Marines. After withdrawal of this diversionary force, the 2d

Marines returned to Saipan, once again for intensive training, in anticipation of landings on the Japanese home islands.

At the war's end the regiment landed at Nagasaki, for occupation duty. After nine months, the 2d Marines relocated to Camp Lejeune, North Carolina, during June and July 1946. By late 1946 the regiment had an advanced amphibious training program underway, but on 19 November 1947, the 2d Marines was reduced to battalion strength, with the designation "2d Marines" kept intact. Upon the request of the Navy for a battalion-sized unit to be deployed with the Sixth Fleet in the Mediterranean Sea, the 2d Marines embarked on 5 January 1948 for the island of Malta. As part of the first amphibious unit to reinforce the Sixth Fleet, the 2d Marines took part in landing exercises until relieved in March. The regiment returned to Camp Lejeune, where it regained two-battalion strength on 17 October 1949.

During the 1950s, the regiment engaged in numerous training exercises in the Caribbean and Mediterranean. From 31 October to 3 November 1956, Battalion Landing Team 3/2 assisted in the evacuation of United States observers and other

Marines of the 81mm Mortar Platoon, attached to the 2d Battalion, 2d Marines, man positions overlooking the city of Beirut, Lebanon, in August 1958.

Department of Defense Photo (USMC) A17465

foreign nationals from Alexandria and the Gaza Strip, as war threatened between Egypt and Israel.

In the summer of 1958, political tensions increased in Lebanon. President Dwight D. Eisenhower, complying with a request from the Lebanese president, decided to intervene with military force. Battalion Landing Team 2/2 made the initial landing in Lebanon on 15 July 1958. When tensions began to ease, the Marines withdrew on 15 August. By 23 October, the unit had returned to Camp Lejeune.

In October 1962, after President John F. Kennedy's ultimatum that Soviet offensive missiles be removed from Cuba, the 2d Battalion and other elements of the 2d Marines embarked once again. They sailed for the Caribbean as part of a larger task force ordered to impose a naval quarantine against arms shipments to Cuba. After the crisis had subsided, the Marines returned to Camp Lejeune in early December.

In late April 1965, internal problems in the Dominican Republic led to intervention by forces of the United States. As part of a joint task force, Battalion Landing Team 1/2 sailed on 1 May and remained offshore as a floating reserve for one month.

Through the 1970s and into the 1980s, the 2d Marines continued to deploy units in a high state of readiness for a wide variety of training exercises and contingency responses. With the advent of the Corps' Unit Deployment Program in 1982, the regiment assumed a truly worldwide posture, periodically deploying battalions to the Pacific for the first time since World War II.

During the 1980s, the 2d Marines took part in many training exercises, which included participation in North Atlantic Treaty Organization exercises, in order to maintain the regiment's traditional high standards of operational readiness.

The Iraqi invasion of Kuwait in August 1990 threatened the stability of the entire Persian Gulf region, and President George H. Bush immediately ordered American forces to the area in order to prevent a possible Iraqi invasion of Saudi Arabia. On 23 August, the 2d Battalion, 2d Marines, was assigned to the operational control of the 6th Marines, and subsequently deployed with that regiment in late December to Saudi Arabia for participation in Operation Desert Shield.

The 2d Marine Division, meanwhile, assigned Regimental Landing Team 2 (RLT 2) to the operational control of the 4th Marine Expeditionary Brigade (4th MEB). During mid-August, RLT 2, consisting of the 1st and 3d Battalions, 2d Marines, along with supporting ground units and aviation

A simulated guerrilla village is searched as part of a training exercise held in Guantanamo Bay, Cuba, by Marines of Company E, 2d Battalion, 2d Marines, on 12 August 1966.

Department of Defense Photo (USMC) A452020

Department of Defense Photo (USN) DN-ST-92-07339

A convoy of cargo trucks of the 1st Battalion, 2d Marines, crosses the desert in Saudi Arabia during Operation Desert Shield.

assets, deployed to the Persian Gulf as part of 4th MEB for participation in Operation Desert Shield. In late September, the two battalions participated in training and amphibious rehearsals for possible employment as a landing force along the Kuwaiti coast. In early January 1991, elements of the 1st Battalion, 2d Marines participated in the evacuation of American civilians and other foreign nationals during Operation Eastern Exit in Somalia. The Battalion Landing Team then returned to the Persian Gulf region to continue planning for contingency operations.

On 24 February, RLT 2's ships sailed north into the Persian Gulf to await tasking, prior to the beginning of the ground portion of Operation Desert Storm. Contingency planning and last minute plans for an amphibious landing in Kuwait continued. With the announcement, however, of the 28 February ceasefire, it was realized that the call for an amphibious landing in Kuwait would not occur. In mid-March, RLT 2 sailed for home,

and was briefed and congratulated by the Commanding General, 4th MEB, on its critical role during Operation Desert Storm in deceiving Iraqi forces as to a possible amphibious landing in Kuwait. The RLT's sister battalion, the 2d Battalion, 2d Marines, participated, however, in the ground assault portion of Operation Desert Storm.

By 23 February, the battalion had moved to its final assembly area prior to the major Allied Coalition assault. On 24 February, the 2d Battalion, 2d Marines, was among the units leading the 2d Marine Division assault into Kuwait, by breaching the center sector of the Iraqi minefields and subsequent defensive lines. Throughout the three-day attack, the battalion met and overcame every challenge and obstacle that was encountered. A 28 February ceasefire ended the fighting, with Iraqi forces thoroughly defeated. In late March, the battalion moved back to Al Jubayl, Saudi Arabia, and returned home to Camp Lejeune in April to a warm welcome.

Meanwhile, on 23 March, the USS *Shreveport* (LPD-12), carrying RLT 2, transited the Suez Canal and entered the Mediterranean Sea, enroute to Rota, Spain. On 15 April, RLT 2 arrived at Morehead City, North Carolina, and was greeted by an enthusiastic and supportive crowd which lined the docks to show its appreciation and to welcome the Marines back home. On 6 May the RLT reverted to the operational command of the 2d Marine Division.

During the remainder of the decade, the 2d Marines participated in operations in locales as diverse as the Caribbean, Africa, and Europe. Elements of the regiment deployed during the 1990s to Cuba, Haiti, Liberia, Somalia, Sierre Leone, Zaire, and Albania. The 2d Marines' versatility and rapid response capability in these operations, which included disaster and humanitarian relief, along with non-combatant emergency evacuations, and support for civil authority, demonstrated the regiment's historic versatility and operational readiness.

Department of Defense Photo (USMC) M-0012-DSP-94-A00320
LCpl J. T. Eimer of Company E, 2d Battalion, 2d Marines, stands at his security post in Cap Haitien, Haiti, in support of Operation Uphold Democracy in September 1994.

2d Marines
Commanding Officers

LtCol Charles G. Long . . . . 19 June 1913 - 5 May 1914
Col James E. Mahoney . . . . .6 May 1914 - 4 December 1914
LtCol Charles G. Long . . . . 5 December 1914 - 7 August 1915
Col Theodore P. Kane . . . . 8 August 1915 - 15 August 1915
Col Eli K. Cole . . . . .16 August 1915 - 8 May 1916

LtCol Laurence H. Moses . . . . 9 May 1916 - 24 June 1916
Col Eli K. Cole . . . . 25 June 1916 - 30 November 1916
LtCol Philip M. Bannon . . . . 1 December 1916 - 10 January 1918
Maj Richard S. Hooker . . . . 11 January 1918 - 31 March 1918
Maj John W. Wadleigh . . . . 1 April 1918 - 28 April 1918

LtCol Richard S. Hooker . . . . 29 April 1918 - 14 November 1918
LtCol Thomas H. Brown . . . . 15 November 1918 - 28 November 1918
LtCol Richard S. Hooker . . . . 29 November 1918 - 9 December 1918
Maj Henry S. Green . . . . 10 December 1918 - 17 January 1919
LtCol Richard S. Hooker . . . . 18 January 1919 - 20 July 1919

LtCol Thomas H. Brown . . . . 21 July 1919 - 10 September 1919
Maj Charles A. Lutz . . . . 11 September 1919 - 2 October 1919
Col Randolph C. Berkeley . . . . 3 October 1919 - 20 October 1921
Col George Van Orden . . . . 21 Ocobert 1921 - 8 April 1923
LtCol William H. Pritchett . . . . 9 April 1923 - 9 July 1923

Col William N. McKelvy . . . . .10 July 1923 - 10 November 1924
Maj Maurice E. Shearer . . . . 11 November 1924 - 9 January 1925
Col William N. McKelvy . . . . .10 January 1925 - 10 June 1925
Maj Maurice E. Shearer . . . . 11 June 1925 - 30 June 1925
Col Harold C. Snyder . . . . .1 July 1925 - 8 April 1926

Col Macker Babb . . . . 9 April 1926 - 30 June 1927
Maj Archibald Young . . . . 1 July 1927 - 19 August 1927
Col Presley M. Rixey II . . . . 20 August 1927 - 21 May 1929
Col Richard P. Williams . . . . 22 May 1929 - 30 May 1930
Col Edward B. Manwaring . . . . 31 May 1930 - 15 May 1932

Col Henry G. Bartlett . . . . 16 May 1932 - 16 June 1932
Col James T. Buttrick . . . . 17 June 1932 - 27 December 1933
Col Eli T. Fryer . . . . 28 December 1933 - 31 May 1934
Maj Samuel P. Budd . . . . 1 June 1934 - 15 August 1934
Col Joseph C. Fegan . . . . 1 February 1941 - 24 October 1941

LtCol Roy C. Swink . . . . 25 October 1941 - 20 November 1941
Col John M. Arthur . . . . 21 November 1941 - 6 June 1943
Col William M. Marshall . . . . 7 June 1943 - 18 July 1943
LtCol Arnold F. Johnston . . . . 19 July 1943 - 26 September 1943
Col William M. Marshall . . . . 27 September 1943 - 7 November 1943

Col David M. Shoup	8 November 1943 - 23 December 1943
LtCol Lloyd Russell	24 December 1943 - 1 January 1944
LtCol Walter J. Stuart	2 January 1944 - 3 September 1944
Col Richard M. Cutts, Jr.	4 September 1944 - 24 October 1945
LtCol Clarence J. O'Donnell	25 October 1945 - 17 April 1946
LtCol Ronald B. Wilde	18 April 1946 - 1 August 1946
Col Francis H. Brink	2 August 1946 - 6 April 1948
LtCol Max C. Chapman	7 April 1948 - 30 April 1948
LtCol Wilbur F. Meyerhoff	1 May 1948 - 18 May 1948
Col Randall M. Victory	19 May 1948 - 21 November 1948
LtCol Harold Granger	22 November 1948 - 31 July 1949
LtCol Jack W. Hawkins	1 August 1949 - 2 October 1949
Col Randall M. Victory	3 October 1949 - 1 February 1950
LtCol Gould P. Groves	2 February 1950 - 25 February 1950
Col Reynolds H. Hayden	26 February 1950 - 28 April 1950
LtCol Gould P. Groves	29 April 1950 - 10 August 1950
LtCol Walter F. Layer	11 August 1950 - 5 September 1950
Col Reynolds H. Hayden	6 September 1950 - 20 July 1951
Col Bruno Hochmuth	21 July 1951 - 29 July 1952
Col Robert F. Scott	30 July 1952 - 16 August 1953
LtCol William A. Stiles	17 August 1953 - 19 October 1953
Col David W. Stonecliffe	20 October 1953 - 9 July 1954
Col George W. Hayes	10 July 1954 - 24 August 1955
Col William R. Collins	25 August 1955 - 5 July 1956
Col Robert E. Cushman, Jr.	6 July 1956 - 19 February 1957
Col Raymond L. Dean	20 February 1957 - 15 July 1957
LtCol Tillman N. Peters	16 July 1957 - 1 August 1957
Col John J. Gormley	2 August 1957 - 25 June 1958
Col Charles R. Baker	26 June 1958 - 1 December 1959
Col Erma A. Wright	2 December 1959 - 12 June 1960
Col Charles W. Kelly, Jr.	13 June 1960 - 16 June 1961
Col Alfred L. Booth	17 June 1961 - 4 April 1962
Col Robert M. Richards	5 April 1962 - 2 July 1963
LtCol John B. Bristow	3 July 1963 - 31 July 1963
Col James Taul	1 August 1963 - 1 August 1964
Col Paul M. Smith	2 August 1964 - 6 Februsry 1965
Col Charles H. Brush, Jr.	7 February 1965 - 7 June 1966
Col William R. Burgoyne, Jr.	8 June 1966 - 31 August 1967
Col Leroy V. Corbett	1 September 1967 - 18 February 1968
Col William E. Barber	19 February 1968 - 13 May 1969
Col Lawrence J. Bradley	14 May 1969 - 28 May 1970
LtCol David M. Twomey	29 May 1970 - 2 March 1971
Col Charles D. Redman	3 March 1971 - 21 April 1972
Col Alfred M. Gray, Jr.	22 April 1972 - 27 December 1972
Col James W. Marsh	28 December 1972 - 18 December 1973

Col James K. Coody . . . . 19 December 1973 - 14 July 1974
Col John E. Greenwood . . . . 15 July 1974 - 30 September 1975
Col Harold L. Blanton, Jr. . . . . 1 October 1975 - 23 June 1977
Col Gerald H. Turley . . . . 24 June 1977 - 21 November 1978
Col Pasquale L. Cacace . . . . 22 November 1978 - 29 May 1980

Col John B. Donovan . . . . 30 May 1980 - 26 March 1981
Col Carl E. Mundy, Jr. . . . . 27 March 1981 - 30 April 1982
Col Robert F. Milligan . . . . 1 May 1982 - 13 May 1983
Col John A. Speicher . . . . 14 May 1983 - 31 May 1984
Col Harry W. Jenkins, Jr. . . . . 1 June 1984 - 8 June 1986

Col Michael J. Bryon . . . . 9 June 1986 - 13 July 1988
Col John W. Ripley . . . . 14 July 1988 - 19 July 1990
Col Tom A. Hobbs . . . . 20 July 1990 - 12 June 1992
Col Richard F. Vercauteren . . . . 13 June 1992 - 16 June 1993
Col Thomas S. Jones . . . . 17 June 1993 - 21 June 1995

LtCol Dennis W. Reilly . . . . 22 June 1995 - 10 August 1995
Col John F. Sattler . . . . 11 August 1995 - 29 May 1997
Col Gordon C. Nash . . . . 30 May 1997 - 30 June 1998
Col Dirk R. Ahle . . . . 1 July 1998 - 21 June 2000
Col Jerry L. Durrant . . . . 22 June 2000 -

2d Marines
LINEAGE

1913 - 1934

ACTIVATED 19 JUNE 1913 AT PHILADELPHIA, PENNSYLVANIA, AS 1ST ADVANCE BASE REGIMENT

REDESIGNATED 23 DECEMBER 1913 AS 1ST ADVANCE BASE REGIMENT, ADVANCE BASE BRIGADE

REDESIGNATED 18 FEBRUARY 1914 AS 1ST REGIMENT, ADVANCE BASE BRIGADE

PARTICIPATED IN THE LANDING AT VERACRUZ, MEXICO, APRIL-NOVEMBER 1914

RELOCATED DURING AUGUST 1915 TO CAP HAITIEN, HAITI

REDESIGNATED 1 JULY 1916 AS 2D REGIMENT, 1ST BRIGADE

REDESIGNATED 1 JANUARY 1933 AS 2D MARINES, 1ST BRIGADE

DEACTIVATED 15 AUGUST 1934

1941 - 1946

REACTIVATED 1 FEBRUARY 1941 AT SAN DIEGO, CALIFORNIA, AS 2D MARINES,
2D MARINE DIVISION

DEPLOYED DURING JULY 1942 TO KORO ISLAND

PARTICIPATED IN THE FOLLOWING WORLD WAR II CAMPAIGNS

GUADALCANAL
TARAWA
SAIPAN
TINIAN
OKINAWA

REDEPLOYED DURING SEPTEMBER 1945 TO NAGASAKI, JAPAN

PARTICIPATED IN THE OCCUPATION OF JAPAN, SEPTEMBER 1945 - JUNE 1946

RELOCATED DURING JUNE-JULY 1946 TO CAMP LEJEUNE, NORTH CAROLINA

1947 - 1989

ELEMENTS PARTICIPATED IN THE LANDINGS IN LEBANON, JULY-AUGUST 1958

PARTICIPATED IN THE CUBAN MISSILE CRISIS, OCTOBER-DECEMBER 1962

ELEMENTS PARTICIPATED IN THE INTERVENTION IN THE DOMINICAN REPUBLIC, MAY 1965

PARTICIPATED IN NUMEROUS TRAINING EXERCISES THROUGHOUT
THE 1970S AND 1980S

1990 - 1999

PARTICIPATED IN OPERATIONS DESERT SHIELD AND DESERT STORM,
SOUTHWEST ASIA, DECEMBER 1990 - APRIL 1991

ELEMENT PARTICIPATED IN HAITIAN REFUGEE OPERATION, CUBA, MAY-JUNE 1992

ELEMENT PARTICIPATED IN OPERATIONS IN SOMALIA, MARCH-AUGUST 1993

ELEMENT PARTICIPATED IN OPERATIONS PROVIDE PROMISE AND DENY FLIGHT, BOSNIA,
AUGUST 1994

ELEMENT PARTICIPATED IN OPERATIONS SUPPORT DEMOCRACY AND UPHOLD DEMOCRACY, HAITI,
AUGUST-OCTOBER 1994

ELEMENTS PARTICIPATED IN OPERATION SEA SIGNAL, CUBA,
SEPTEMBER-DECEMBER 1994 AND JULY-OCTOBER 1995

ELEMENT PARTICIPATED IN OPERATION ASSURED RESPONSE, LIBERIA,
APRIL-JUNE 1996

2d Marines
HONORS

PRESIDENTIAL UNIT CITATION STREAMER WITH ONE BRONZE STAR

WORLD WAR II
GUADALCANAL - 1942
TARAWA - 1943

NAVY UNIT COMMENDATION STREAMER

SOUTHWEST ASIA
1990 - 1991

MEXICAN SERVICE STREAMER

HAITIAN CAMPAIGN STREAMER WITH ONE BRONZE STAR

MARINE CORPS EXPEDITIONARY STREAMER WITH ONE BRONZE STAR

WORLD WAR I VICTORY STREAMER WITH "WEST INDIES"

AMERICAN DEFENSE SERVICE STREAMER

ASIATIC-PACIFIC CAMPAIGN STREAMER WITH ONE SILVER AND ONE BRONZE STAR

WORLD WAR II VICTORY STREAMER

NAVY OCCUPATION SERVICE STREAMER WITH "ASIA" AND "EUROPE"

NATIONAL DEFENSE SERVICE STREAMER WITH TWO BRONZE STARS

ARMED FORCES EXPEDITIONARY STREAMER WITH TWO BRONZE STARS

SOUTHWEST ASIA SERVICE STREAMER WITH TWO BRONZE STARS

The 6th Marines

The 6th Marines was organized on 11 July 1917 at Quantico, Virginia, for combat service with the American Expeditionary Force in France. Commanded by Colonel Albertus W. Catlin, the regiment was composed of the following units: the 1st Battalion, consisting of the 74th, 75th, 76th, and 95th Companies; the 2d Battalion, consisting of the 78th, 79th, 80th, and 96th Companies; and the 3d

Battalion, consisting of the 82d, 83d, 84th, and 97th Companies. The regiment spent the summer of 1917 in extensive training and maneuvers at Quantico, conducting drills in trench and gas warfare, and the use of hand grenades, the bayonet, and machine guns.

In less than eight months, the regiment was fighting on the front lines in France. The 5th and

A contingent of 6th Marines passes in review on 8 August 1919, as the 2d Division parades up 5th Avenue from Washington Square, New York City.

National Archives Photo (USMC) 127-N-519458

30

6th Marines, along with the 6th Machine Gun Battalion, formed the 4th Marine Brigade commanded by Brigadier General Charles A. Doyen. As part of the U.S. Army's 2d Infantry Division, the 4th Marine Brigade participated in some of the heaviest fighting of World War I.

In a series of bitterly contested battles during 6-25 June 1918, the 6th Marines helped to sweep German troops from Belleau Wood, receiving along with the 5th Marines, special commendation from the French Government. The Belleau Wood area was renamed "Bois de la Brigade de Marine."

Shortly after the engagement at Belleau Wood, the 6th Marines fought at Soissons, suffering heavy casualties from German artillery and machine gun fire. By the end of July 1918, however, the German line had been broken, bringing about the capture of hundreds of guns and thousands of prisoners.

The 6th Marines then moved to a rest and training area, to prepare for the St. Mihiel offensive, which began on 12 November 1918. In this operation the 2d Infantry Division was commanded by Marine Major General John A. Lejeune. The 6th Marines again displayed tenacity and coolness under fire, while driving back a determined enemy.

During October 1918, the 6th Marines participated in the Meuse-Argonne drive. In a series of assaults and counterattacks, the regiment captured the fortified hill of Blanc Mont and the heights of St. Etienne, freeing the Allied approaches to the western Argonne. In the closing weeks of the war, the 6th Marines also took part in the final phase of the Meuse-Argonne drive, and on 10 November 1918, one day before the signing of the Armistice, succeeded in crossing the Meuse River. Two Marines of the regiment received the Medal of Honor: Corporal John H. Pruitt, 78th Company, and Gunnery Sergeant Fred W. Stockham, 96th Company. At the conclusion of World War I the French Government awarded three unit decorations, including the coveted Croix de Guerre with Palm, to the 6th Marines.

After the Armistice, the regiment crossed the Rhine River to serve for a short while in occupied Germany. Redeploying in July 1919, it returned to Quantico, where it was disbanded on 13 August 1919.

Two years later, on 15 September 1921, the 6th Marines was reactivated at Quantico, for a varied history of service with the East Coast Expeditionary Force, overseas duty in China, and maneuvers with the Fleet Marine Force—all interspersed with periods of disbandment or inactivation.

Elements of the 6th Marines served briefly at Guantanamo Bay, Cuba, and landed in the Dominican Republic during the 1920s to protect American interests. For the most part, however, the regiment's postwar duties focused on training and maneuvers.

In May 1927, when American lives and property in China were threatened, the 6th Marines deployed quickly to Shanghai as part of the 3d Brigade, to help defend the city's International Settlement. The regiment's next two years in China consisted mainly of guard and patrol duty. Early in 1929 the 6th Marines withdrew from the Far East, and returned to San Diego, California, where it disbanded on 31 March 1929.

Upon the establishment of the Fleet Marine Force, the 6th Marines was reactivated on 1 September 1934 at San Diego. The regiment took part in Pacific maneuvers with the U.S. Fleet in the spring of 1935, before returning to San Diego for further training and exercises. During the summer of 1937, more trouble in China caused another deployment in the Far East. The 6th Marines sailed for Shanghai in September 1937, to augment American forces already positioned in the International Settlement. The regiment returned to the United States in April 1938 and assumed an inactive status.

In March 1940, the 6th Marines was reestablished at Marine Corps Base, San Diego. The regiment became the principal infantry unit of the 2d Marine Brigade, which on 1 February 1941, was

Two Marines stand guard at an observation post of the 2d Battalion, 6th Marines, in Shanghai, China, in 1937.

National Archives Photo (USMC) 127G-A521056

Department of Defense Photo (USMC) A524213

A squad of infantrymen from the 6th Marines train in wind-swept, snow-covered fields in a period of half-light during the Icelandic winter in 1941-1942.

redesignated the 2d Marine Division. During the summer of 1941, the 6th Marines was temporarily detached from the division when it was incorporated, along with other Marine units, into the 1st Provisional Marine Brigade. The regiment deployed to Iceland with the brigade, to preclude a threatened German invasion. Upon its return from Iceland in March 1942, the 6th Marines again was stationed at San Diego, and reassigned to the 2d Marine Division.

On 19 October 1942, the 6th Marines began deploying to New Zealand, enroute to rejoining other 2d Marine Division units on Guadalcanal. By mid-January 1943, the regiment had assumed frontline positions in the right half of the 2d Marine Division's sector. The 6th Marines, along with Army units, assaulted Japanese defenses in that area, and in the sectors east and south of Kokumbona. Relieved of frontline duty on 30 January, the regiment continued to assist in mopping-up operations on the island. In early February 1943, the 6th Marines and other units of the 2d Marine Division left Guadalcanal for New Zealand to undergo reha-

bilitation and training in preparation for the Gilbert Islands campaign.

At Tarawa Atoll, on 20 November 1943, the 6th Marines was initially held in reserve. But the precarious position of the 2d Marine Division at the end of the first day's fighting soon required its reserve to be committed to the battle. The 1st Battalion, 6th Marines, landed on Betio Island on 21 November 1943. That afternoon, the 2d Battalion, 6th Marines, landed on Bairiki Island, east of Betio, and seized the island. The Japanese avenue of retreat from Tarawa was now blocked, and the Marine seizure of Bairiki provided an excellent location from which Marine artillery could support operations on Betio. By the following day most of the regiment's men were heavily engaged against strongly defended Japanese pillboxes and artillery on Betio. The island was declared secure on 23 November, and all three battalions of the 6th Marines spent the following days in cleaning out the rest of the atoll. By 28 November, all of Tarawa was in American hands. The 2d Marine Division subsequently relocated to Hawaii during Decem-

Department of Defense Photo (USMC) A64032

Marines move out from the beachhead onto the smoke-covered Japanese airstrip on Tarawa in November 1943.

ber 1943, to begin preparation for its next amphibious operation.

The 6th Marines played a paramount role in the assault on the Marianas during the summer of 1944. The regiment landed on the southwest coast of Saipan on 15 June 1944, with troops of the 2d and 4th Marine Divisions, and advanced inland despite determined enemy resistance. The 6th Marines fought off savage Japanese counterattacks during the night of 16-17 June, and again on 26 June. After recapturing the town of Garapan, on 4 July, the 2d Marine Division briefly went into reserve, but soon rejoined the steady, but slow, advance against a system of well-defended caves. Organized Japanese resistance on Saipan virtually ceased on the island by 8 July. On that day the 2d Marine Division replaced the Army's 27th Division in the front lines, and continued to mop up remaining groups of Japanese holdouts on the island.

The 2d and 4th Divisions landed on Tinian on 24 July 1944, and advanced rapidly inland. The 6th Marines participated in the steady drive southward on Tinian, which by 31 July had brought the regiment to a line of vertical cliffs, where Japanese resistance had stiffened. Fighting alongside the 8th

Marines, the 6th Marines repulsed several enemy counterattacks. By 1 August, organized resistance had ceased, although sporadic clashes continued for another week. The 6th Marines returned to

BGen Merritt A. Edson, assistant division commander of the 2d Marine Division, confers with Col James P. Risely, commanding officer of the 6th Marines, and LtCol Kenneth F. McLeod, executive officer of the 6th Marines, on Saipan during June 1944.

Department of Defense Photo (USMC) A82481

Deparment of Defense Photo (USMC) A152074

Supported by a medium tank, Marines advance on Tinian during late July 1944.

Saipan in mid-August, where it took part in mopping-up operations, which would include a major drive in November.

The 2d Marine Division left Saipan for Okinawa in late March 1945. On D-Day, 1 April, the 6th Marines engaged in diversionary activities along the southeast coast of the island. The 2d Marine Division remained in floating reserve. The 130th Naval Construction Battalion and the 2d Amphibian Truck Company were put ashore on 11 April, and the remainder of the division returned to Saipan. Later, in June, the 8th Marines and reinforcing units went back to Okinawa and took part in the final days of fighting.

After the Japanese surrender, the 6th Marines accompanied the 2d Marine Division to Japan. The regiment arrived at Nagasaki on 23 September 1945 for occupation duty. It left Japan during June 1946, but in lieu of rejoining the 2d Marine Division units at Camp Lejeune, North Carolina, it was relocated instead to Camp Pendleton,

California, where it was attached to the 3d Marine Brigade on 11 September 1946. Upon the deactivation of the 3d Marine Brigade the following year, the 6th Marines was transferred to the 1st Marine Division. The regiment was deactivated on 1 October 1949; on 17 October, however, a new 6th Marines was activated as part of the 2d Marine Division at Camp Lejeune, North Carolina.

The outbreak of the fighting in Korea in July 1950 created an immediate need to build up the understrength 1st Marine Division. This brought about further changes in the organizational structure of the 6th Marines. Organic units of the regiment were transferred to the 1st and 7th Marines, 1st Marine Division. Within days, however, new elements of the 6th Marines were activated. The regiment was quickly brought up to wartime strength, underwent an intensive training program, and soon resumed its place as one of the major combat elements of the 2d Marine Division.

Since January 1950, the 6th Marines has provid-

Department of Defense Photo (USMC) A19986

Personnel of the 1st Battalion, 6th Marines, gathered on the airfield in Santo Domingo, Dominican Republic, in May 1965.

ed reinforced battalions, on a rotating basis, for service with the U.S. Sixth Fleet in the Mediterranean. In July 1958, after an urgent appeal from Lebanon, President Dwight D. Eisenhower ordered American troops into Beirut, to support the Lebanese government. The 3d Battalion, 6th Marines, landed near Beirut on the morning of 16 July 1958 as part of the 2d Provisional Marine Brigade, and remained ashore until 1 October 1958.

During the Cuban missile crisis of October 1962, all elements of the 6th Marines were embarked to assist in the quarantine of Cuba, ready to land if required. In the aftermath of the crisis, 2d Marine Division units remained in the Caribbean area until early December 1962.

Chaotic conditions in the Dominican Republic during April 1965 once more tested the capabilities of the 6th Marines. Elements of the regiment were the first to respond to President Lyndon B. Johnson's orders to deploy Marines into the capital city of Santo Domingo, to protect American lives and property and to assist in evacuations. With the rest of the 4th Marine Expeditionary Brigade, units of the 6th Marines helped in the evacuation of more than 1,300 refugees from the Dominican Republic during April-June 1965, before returning to Camp Lejeune.

During the 1970s and 1980s, units of the 6th Marines conducted numerous amphibious and training exercises, especially in the Mediterranean and the Caribbean. As part of the 22d Marine Amphibious Unit, the 2d Battalion, 6th Marines—as the nucleus of Battalion Landing Team 2/6—deployed to Beirut, Lebanon, during February-June 1983, as part of a multinational peacekeeping force.

The next test of the regiment's operational readiness occurred in December 1989, when elements of the 6th Marines participated in Operation Just Cause in Panama. This operation was launched to protect American lives, restore the democratic process, and preserve the integrity of the Panama Canal Treaty. The operation concluded in June 1990.

Barely two months after the termination of Operation Just Cause, the readiness of the 6th Marines was again put to the test. In August 1990, the forces of Iraqi dictator Saddam Hussein invad-

Marines of Company K, 3d Battalion, 6th Marines, man a roadblock that separated Howard Air Force Base from the coastal town of Vera Cruz, Panama, during Operation Just Cause in 1990.

ed Kuwait, sparking a major crisis in the Persian Gulf. After President George H. Bush ordered American military forces to the region, the 6th Marines immediately underwent an aggressive training program. As preparations continued at a rapid pace at Camp Lejeune for possible deployment to Southwest Asia, there was still work to be done on the regiment's organization. The 2d Battalion, 6th Marines, had been deactivated in 1989, and its place in the regiment was taken by the 2d Battalion, 2d Marines. In November, the 2d Marine Division received the anticipated orders for deployment to the Persian Gulf, and in mid-December, the 6th Marines deployed to Saudi Arabia for Operation Desert Shield.

It was quickly recognized that whatever mission might be assigned, the ability to move into Kuwait to engage the enemy would depend on the ability of the 2d Marine Division to conduct a successful breach of Iraqi defenses. By early February, it was determined that the division's breach of these defenses would be conducted by the 6th Marines, as that regiment had the most training in breaching operations.

Early on the morning of 24 February 1991, the 6th Marines, with attached combat engineers, assaulted the Iraqi defensive lines, using mine plows, mine rakes, and line charges to blow up the obstacles. Six breach lanes were successfully made through the enemy minefields. The following day, the 6th Marines was engaged by an Iraqi battalion-sized armor and mechanized infantry force. Fighting back with its own tanks and air support, the regiment routed the enemy. As Iraqi forces began to surrender in large numbers, the regiment continued movement to its assigned objectives. On 28 February, a general ceasefire ended 2d Marine Division offensive operations.

During March, the regiment maintained a defensive posture and continued mopping up operations in the vicinity of Al Jahra, Kuwait, until movement to the south later in the month. During April, the regiment redeployed to North Carolina, and received a hearty welcome at Camp Lejeune for a job well done.

The 6th Marines continued to utilize its skills and team spirit during the 1990s in humanitarian and peacekeeping activities. Elements of the regiment participated from July-October 1994 in support of Operation Sea Signal at Guantanamo Bay, Cuba. The operation was a humanitarian relief effort for 14,000 Haitian migrants seeking shelter from a military dictatorship, and more than 30,000 Cubans stymied by the closing of a door to the United States. More recently, elements of the regiment participated during 1995-96 in Operations Deny Flight and Joint Endeavor in Bosnia; Operations Southern Watch and Desert Thunder in Southwest Asia in 1998; and Operation United Force in Kosovo in 1999. The participation of the 6th Marines in these operations was undertaken in conjunction with other American and foreign forces, in support of United Nations peacekeeping efforts in the strife-torn nations.

At right, members of the 6th Marines disembark from the USS Dubuque *(LPD-8) upon their arrival in Saudi Arabia as part of Operation Desert Shield in September 1990.* (Department of Defense Photo (USN) DN-ST-91-02384) *Below, Marines from Company C, 1st Battalion, 6th Marines, participate in Operation Urban Warrior at Camp Lejeune in January 1998.* (Photo courtesy of 2d Marine Division)

6th Marines
Commanding Officers

Col Albertus W. Catlin . . . . 11 July1917 - 15 November 1917
Maj Frank E. Evans . . . . 16 November 1917 - 15 January 1918
Col Albertus W. Catlin . . . . 16 January 1918 - 6 June 1918
LtCol Harry Lee. . . . . 7 June 1918 - 12 July 1918
Maj Thomas Holcomb . . . . 13 July 1918 - 15 July 1918

LtCol Harry Lee . . . . 16 July 1918 - 12 August 1919
Capt Charles B. Hobbs . . . . 15 December 1920 - 22 March 1921
Capt Francis S. Kieren . . . . 23 March 1921 - 20 July 1921
Maj Calvin B. Matthews . . . . 21 July 1921 - 8 September 1921
Capt Thomas E. Wicks . . . . 22 November 1921 - 6 January 1922

Maj Calvin B. Matthews . . . . 7 January 1922 - 14 August 1922
Maj Harold L. Parsons . . . . 15 August 1922 - 4 September 1922
Maj Calvin B. Matthews . . . . 5 September 1922 - 19 February 1923
Maj Thomas S. Clarke . . . . 20 February 1923 - 31 July 1923
Maj James J. Meade . . . . 1 August 1923 - 8 October 1923

LtCol Edward A. Greene . . . . 9 October 1923 - 25 November 1923
Maj Ralph S. Keyser . . . . 26 November 1923 - 25 February 1924
Maj Howard C. Judson . . . . 26 February 1924 - 4 June 1924
LtCol Edward A. Greene . . . . 5 June 1924 - 15 March 1925
Col Harold C. Snyder . . . . 26 March 1927 - 2 August 1928

Col Charles H. Lyman . . . . 3 August 1928 - 9 January 1929
Maj Calhoun Ancrum . . . . 10 January 1929 - 31 March 1929
LtCol Andrew B. Drum . . . . 1 September 1934 - 30 September 1935
LtCol Oliver Floyd . . . . 1 October 1935 - 30 October 1935
Col Philip H. Torrey . . . . 31 October 1935 - 7 June 1937

Col Thomas S. Clarke . . . . 8 June 1937 - 12 January 1938
LtCol James L. Underhill . . . . 13 January 1938 - 11 May 1938
LtCol Alphonse De Carre . . . . 12 May 1938 - 15 May 1938
Col Harry L. Smith . . . . 16 May 1938 - 31 May 1939
LtCol Earl H. Jenkins . . . . 1 June 1939 - 20 June 1939

Col Samuel L. Howard . . . . 21 June 1939 - 2 June 1940
LtCol Franklin A. Hart . . . . 3 June 1940 - 21 June 1940
LtCol Oliver P. Smith . . . . 22 June 1940 - 28 June 1940
LtCol Franklin A. Hart . . . . 29 June 1940 - 23 July 1940
Col Leo D. Hermle . . . . 24 July 1940 - 31 December 1941

LtCol William McN. Marshall . . . . 1 January 1942 - 24 March 1942
Col Leo D. Hermle . . . . 28 March 1942 - 31 July 1942
Col Gilder D. Jackson, Jr. . . . . 1 August 1942 - 13 April 1943
LtCol Lyman G. Miller . . . . 14 April 1943 - 30 April 1943
Col Maurice G. Holmes . . . . 3 May 1943 - 16 December 1943

Col James P. Riseley .... 17 December 1943 - 3 September 1944
Col Gregon W. Williams .... 4 September 1944 - 5 November 1945
Col Jack P. Juhan .... 6 November 1945 - 24 January 1946
Col James P. Berkeley .... 25 January 1946 - 26 March 1946
Col John F. Hough .... 27 March 1946 - 30 March 1947

Col George H. Potter .... 31 March 1947 - 6 April 1947
Col John F. Hough .... 7 April 1947 - 11 June 1947
LtCol Thomas C. Kerrigan .... 12 June 1947 - 29 June 1947
Col Hewin O. Hammond .... 30 June 1947 - 15 July 1947
Col James P. S. Devereux .... 16 July 1947 - 30 September 1947

Col George H. Potter .... 1 October 1947 - 31 October 1947
Maj Norman R. Nickerson .... 1 November 1947 - 13 November 1947
Col George H. Potter .... 14 November 1947 - 30 April 1948
LtCol George D. Rich .... 1 May 1948 - 23 May 1948
Col George H. Potter .... 24 May 1948 - 6 July 1948

LtCol William N. McGill .... 7 July 1948 - 8 March 1949
Col John H. Cook, Jr. .... 9 March 1949 - 1 October 1949
Col Homer L. Litzenberg, Jr. .... 17 October 1949 - 7 July 1950
Col Russell N. Jordhal .... 8 July 1950 - 13 August 1950
LtCol William F. Prickett .... 14 August 1950 - 10 September 1950

Col Henry W. Buse, Jr. .... 11 September 1950 - 13 December 1951
Col William F. Prickett .... 14 December 1951 - 16 January 1952
Col Ormand R. Simpson .... 17 January 1952 - 23 April 1953
Col Charles M. Nees .... 24 April 1953 - 27 July 1954
Col Jean H. Buckner .... 28 July 1954 - 1 June 1955

LtCol Wilson F. Humphreys .... 2 June 1955 - 9 July 1955
Col Edward L. Hutchinson .... 10 July 1955 - 5 July 1956
Col Max C. Chapman .... 6 July 1956 - 10 June 1957
LtCol Theodore F. Beeman .... 11 June 1957 - 16 July 1957
Col Austin C. Shofner .... 17 July 1957 - 11 August 1958

Col William J. McKennan .... 12 August 1958 - 1 December 1959
Col Melvin D. Henderson .... 2 December 1959 - 7 March 1961
Col Maxie R. Williams .... 8 March 1961 - 6 June 1961
Col Jonas H. Platt .... 10 July 1961 - 19 July 1962
Col Robert W. L. Bross .... 8 August 1962 - 26 July 1963

LtCol Anthony A. Akstin .... 27 July 1963 - 23 August 1963
Col Glenn R. Long .... 24 August 1963 - 13 July 1963
Col George W. E. Daughtry .... 14 July 1963 - 14 July 1965
Col John N. McLaughlin .... 15 July 1965 - 28 December 1965
Col James B. Ord .... 29 December 1965 - 6 July 1966

Col James C. Short .... 7 July 1966 - 1 June 1967
Col Oscar T. Jensen, Jr. .... 2 June 1967 - 11 March 1968
Col Richard H. Kern .... 12 March 1968 - 26 March 1968
Col Robert M. Platt .... 27 March 1968 - 6 August 1969
Col Paul B. Haigwood .... 7 August 1969 - 14 October 1970

Col Francis R. Kraince . . . . 15 October 1970 - 1 June 1972
LtCol John J. Peeler . . . . 2 June 1972 - 19 March 1973
Col Ezra H. Arkland . . . . 20 March 1973 - 20 February 1974
Col David M. Ridderhof . . . . 21 February 1974 - 7 May 1975
Col Harold G. Glasgow . . . . 8 May 1975 - 3 June 1976

Col Daniel J. Ford . . . . 4 June 1976 - 23 September 1977
Col Leemon B. McHenry . . . . 24 September 1977 - 18 July 1978
Col Francis V. White, Jr. . . . . 19 July 1978 - 20 June 1979
Col Louis J. Piantadosi . . . . 21 June 1979 - 19 May 1980
Col Frederic L. Tolleson . . . . 20 May 1980 - 20 August 1981

Col Randall W. Austin . . . . 21 August 1981 - 19 October 1983
Col William M. Keys . . . . 20 October 1983 - 7 February 1986
Col James E. Livingston . . . . 8 February 1986 - 24 June 1987
Col John J. Carroll . . . . 25 June 1987 - 8 August 1988
Col Russell H. Sutton . . . . 9 August 1988 - 12 June 1990

Col Lawrence H. Livingston . . . . 13 June 1990 - 27 February 1992
Col James H. Benson . . . . 28 February 1992 - 15 July 1993
Col Richard A. Huck . . . . 16 July 1993 - 9 June 1995
Col James C. Hardee . . . . 10 June 1995 - 23 July 1997
Col Thomas E. Sheets . . . . 24 July 1997 - 9 July 1998

Col Robert G. Neller . . . . 10 July 1998 - 6 July 2000
Col John C. Coleman . . . . 7 July 2000 -

6th Marines
LINEAGE

1917 - 1921

ACTIVATED 11 JULY 1917 AT QUANTICO, VIRGINIA, AS THE 6TH REGIMENT

DEPLOYED DURING OCTOBER 1917 - FEBRUARY 1918 TO FRANCE, AND ASSIGNED TO THE 4TH MARINE BRIGADE, 2D DIVISION (ARMY), AMERICAN EXPEDITIONARY FORCE

PARTICIPATED IN THE FOLLOWING WORLD WAR I OFFENSIVE CAMPAIGNS

AISNE
AISNE-MARNE
ST. MIHIEL
MEUSE-ARGONNE

PARTICIPATED IN THE FOLLOWING WORLD WAR I DEFENSIVE CAMPAIGNS

TOULON-TROYON
CHATEAU-THIERRY
MARBACHE
LIMEY

PARTICIPATED IN THE OCCUPATION OF THE GERMAN RHINELAND,
DECEMBER 1918 - JULY 1919

RELOCATED DURING AUGUST 1919 TO QUANTICO, VIRGINIA

ELEMENT OF THE REGIMENT REMAINED ON ACTIVE DUTY, 1919-1921

1921 - 1925

REACTIVATED 15 SEPTEMBER 1921 AT QUANTICO, VIRGINIA

ELEMENTS PARTICIPATED IN EXPEDITIONARY DUTY IN CUBA AND THE
DOMINICAN REPUBLIC, JUNE 1924 - MARCH 1925

DEACTIVATED 15 MARCH 1925 AT QUANTICO, VIRGINIA

1927 - 1929

REACTIVATED 26 MARCH 1927 AT PHILADELPHIA, PENNSYLVANIA

DEPLOYED DURING MAY 1927 TO SHANGHAI, CHINA, AND ASSIGNED TO
THE 3D BRIGADE

RELOCATED DURING MARCH 1929 TO SAN DIEGO, CALIFORNIA, AND
DETACHED FROM THE 3D BRIGADE

DEACTIVATED 31 MARCH 1929

1934 - 1949

REACTIVATED 1 SEPTEMBER 1934 AT SAN DIEGO, CALIFORNIA, AS THE
6TH MARINES, FLEET MARINE FORCE

ASSIGNED 1 JULY 1936 TO THE 2D MARINE BRIGADE, FLEET MARINE FORCE

DEPLOYED DURING SEPTEMBER 1937 TO SHANGHAI, CHINA

RELOCATED DURING APRIL 1938 TO SAN DIEGO, CALIFORNIA

2D MARINE BRIGADE REDESIGNATED 1 FEBRUARY 1941 AS THE 2D MARINE DIVISION, FLEET
MARINE FORCE

DEPLOYED DURING MAY-JULY 1941 TO REYKJAVIK, ICELAND, AND ASSIGNED
TO THE 1ST PROVISIONAL MARINE BRIGADE

RELOCATED DURING FEBRUARY-MARCH 1942 TO SAN DIEGO, CALIFORNIA,
AND REASSIGNED TO THE 2D MARINE DIVISION, FLEET MARINE FORCE

DEPLOYED DURING OCTOBER-NOVEMBER 1942 TO WELLINGTON,
NEW ZEALAND

PARTICIPATED IN THE FOLLOWING WORLD WAR II CAMPAIGNS

GUADALCANAL
SOUTHERN SOLOMONS
TARAWA
SAIPAN
TINIAN
OKINAWA

DEPLOYED DURING SEPTEMBER 1945 TO NAGASAKI, JAPAN

PARTICIPATED IN THE OCCUPATION OF JAPAN, SEPTEMBER 1945 - JUNE 1946

RELOCATED DURING JULY 1946 TO CAMP PENDLETON, CALIFORNIA

REASSIGNED 11 SEPTEMBER 1946 TO THE 3D MARINE BRIGADE,
FLEET MARINE FORCE

REASSIGNED 11 JULY 1947 TO THE 1ST MARINE DIVISION,
FLEET MARINE FORCE

DEACTIVATED 1 OCTOBER 1949

1949 - 1988

REACTIVATED 17 OCTOBER 1949 AT CAMP LEJEUNE, NORTH CAROLINA,
AND ASSIGNED TO THE 2D MARINE DIVISION, FLEET MARINE FORCE

ELEMENTS PARTICIPATED IN THE LANDINGS IN LEBANON,
JULY-OCTOBER 1958

PARTICIPATED IN THE CUBAN MISSILE CRISIS, OCTOBER-DECEMBER 1962

ELEMENTS PARTICIPATED IN THE INTERVENTION IN THE DOMINICAN REPUBLIC, APRIL-JUNE 1965

PARTICIPATED IN NUMEROUS TRAINING EXERCISES THROUGHOUT THE 1970S

ELEMENTS PARTICIPATED AS PART OF THE MULTINATIONAL PEACEKEEPING FORCE IN LEBANON,
FEBRUARY-JUNE 1983

1989 - 1999

ELEMENTS DEPLOYED TO PANAMA DURING JANUARY 1989 - JUNE 1990

PARTICIPATED IN OPERATIONS DESERT SHIELD AND DESERT STORM, SOUTHWEST ASIA,
SEPTEMBER 1990 - APRIL 1991

ELEMENTS PARTICIPATED IN SUPPORT OF OPERATION SEA SIGNAL, CUBA, JULY-OCTOBER 1994 AND
OCTOBER-DECEMBER 1995

ELEMENT PARTICIPATED IN SUPPORT OF OPERATIONS DENY FLIGHT AND JOINT ENDEAVOR,
BOSNIA, SEPTEMBER 1995 - FEBRUARY 1996

ELEMENT PARTICIPATED IN OPERATIONS SOUTHERN WATCH AND DESERT THUNDER,
SOUTHWEST ASIA, FEBRUARY-APRIL 1998

ELEMENT PARTICIPATED IN OPERATION UNITED FORCE, KOSOVO, MARCH-APRIL 1999

6th Marines
HONORS

PRESIDENTIAL UNIT CITATION STREAMER

WORLD WAR II
TARAWA - 1943

NAVY UNIT COMMENDATION STREAMER

SOUTHWEST ASIA
1990-1991

WORLD WAR I VICTORY STREAMER WITH ONE SILVER STAR

ARMY OF OCCUPATION OF GERMANY STREAMER

YANGTZE SERVICE STREAMER

MARINE CORPS EXPEDITIONARY STREAMER WITH THREE BRONZE STARS

CHINA SERVICE STREAMER

AMERICAN DEFENSE SERVICE STREAMER WITH ONE BRONZE STAR

EUROPEAN-AFRICAN-MIDDLE EASTERN CAMPAIGN STREAMER

ASIATIC-PACIFIC CAMPAIGN STREAMER WITH ONE SILVER AND ONE BRONZE STAR

WORLD WAR II VICTORY STREAMER

NAVY OCCUPATION SERVICE STREAMER WITH "ASIA" AND "EUROPE"

NATIONAL DEFENSE SERVICE STREAMER WITH TWO BRONZE STARS

ARMED FORCES EXPEDITIONARY STREAMER WITH TWO BRONZE STARS

SOUTHWEST ASIA SERVICE STREAMER WITH TWO BRONZE STARS

FRENCH CROIX DE GUERRE WITH TWO PALMS AND ONE GILT STAR

The 8th Marines

The 8th Marines was originally activated as the 8th Regiment at Quantico, Virginia, on 9 October 1917. The infantry regiment was formed by companies from Philadelphia and California's Mare Island, as well as Quantico. Major Ellis B. Miller, a 37-year-old Iowan, assumed command of the regiment, which had a strength of approximately 1,000.

The outbreak of hostilities between the United States and Germany in 1917 had caused the regiment's activation, but it was first sent to Texas, instead of France. During November 1917, the regiment moved to Fort Crockett, near Galveston, to guard against German agents who might try to disrupt vital shipments from Mexican oil fields. Duties in Texas were those of a typical garrison force, with a training program pointed toward contingency operations in Mexico. The need for such operations never materialized. The regiment embarked on board the USS *Hancock* (AP-3) in April 1919. Upon returning to Philadelphia it was deactivated.

By the end of 1919, however, the 8th Regiment was reactivated in Haiti. At Port-au-Prince, the 1st

Marines near Port-au-Prince, Haiti, in 1920 prepare to patrol in search of Caco bandits.
Deparment of Defense Photo (USMC) A519809

Battalion was activated on 17 December, and the regimental headquarters on 5 January 1920. Lieutenant Colonel Louis McCarty Little, an officer with prior service in Latin America and China, was given command of the reactivated 8th Regiment, which in turn was assigned to the 1st Marine Brigade. During 1920 and 1921, the regiment suppressed Caco bandits in the southern half of the country, primarily in the region around Port-au-Prince. By early 1922, banditry had almost been eradicated in Haiti, and the 8th Regiment soon switched its emphasis to duties related to civic action: mapping the country; helping to construct roads and sanitation facilities; and training the local constabulary. Under continued peaceful conditions, the regiment was deactivated at Port-au-Prince on 1 July 1925.

In early 1940, the Marine Corps gradually began to increase the number of units on active duty, as a consequence of general war in Europe during 1939. The first major organization to be brought back into being was the 8th Marines, reactivated on 1 April 1940 at San Diego, California. Colonel Leo D. Hermle, a veteran of World War I, took command of the regiment, which was initially assigned to the 2d Marine Brigade. The 8th Marines was assigned to the 2d Marine Division at the division's activation on 1 February 1941, and joined other division units in training exercises on San Clemente Island, off the coast of Southern California.

Department of Defense Photo (USMC) A51831
Col Richard H. Jeshke, commanding officer of the 8th Marines, and LtCol Augustus Fricke, commanding the 3d Battalion, 8th Marines, discuss plans for a new drive on Guadalcanal in January 1943.

After the Japanese struck at Pearl Harbor on 7 December, the 8th Marines had an initial mission of defending the California coast from Oceanside to the Mexican border against a possible Japanese at-

Maj Henry P. "Jim" Crowe is at his command post, where he observes and directs the 2d Battalion, 8th Marines, during the bitter fighting on Tawara in late November 1943.

Department of Defense Photo (USMC) A63956

tack. The regiment was next ordered to prepare for deployment to American Samoa, in the South Pacific. Forming the nucleus of a new 2d Marine Brigade, the 8th Marines sailed from California on 6 January 1942—part of the first force to mount out for the Pacific after the outbreak of war. Arriving at the Samoan capital of Pago Pago on 19 January, the regiment, now commanded by Colonel Richard H. Jeschke, took over the job of shoring up the island's defenses from the 7th Defense Battalion.

By summer, the 8th Marines had begun to prepare for offensive operations outside of the Samoan area. The regiment's first combat assignment of World War II came during the struggle for Guadalcanal. On 4 November 1942, after a 10-day voyage from Samoa, the unit reached the embattled island, and went ashore near Lunga Point on the northern coast. Almost immediately, the unit was involved in heavy fighting with the Japanese, which continued through November and into the next month.

During January the 8th Marines, with other Marine Corps and Army units, made a final drive toward the west, with the support of naval gunfire. Guadalcanal was eventually declared secure on 8 February 1943.

The entire regiment reassembled for a period of rest and relaxation in New Zealand on 16 February 1943, establishing a permanent base near Paekakariki, 35 miles north of Wellington. Large quantities of war material began to arrive from the United States. The target for the next campaign was the Gilbert Islands, and the capture of Tarawa Atoll. A significant enemy garrison was located on Betio Island.

Shortly before dawn on 20 November 1943 the transports carrying the invasion force arrived off Betio. The initial wave to go ashore consisted of Major Henry P. "Jim" Crowe's 2d Battalion, 8th Marines, and the 2d and 3d Battalions, 2d Marines. The 3d Battalion, 8th Marines, headed for the beach several hours later, losing many men from enemy machine gun fire, shell fragments, and

Men of the 8th Marines pause to regroup during the battle for Saipan in June 1944.

Department of Defense Photo (USMC) A82703

Department of Defense Photo (USMC) A126987

Men of the 8th Marines on board LSTs advance toward their objective, Iheya Shima, in June 1945, as the small island off Okinawa's northern coast is also assaulted by air.

drownings. When the landing craft were unable to get past an offshore reef, the Marines dismounted and waded ashore, crossing hundreds of yards through a fire-swept lagoon. Early on 21 November the 1st Battalion joined the regiment ashore. The Marines suffered extremely heavy losses during four days of bitter fighting. The 8th Marines, less the 1st Battalion, stood down on 23 November. By the end of that day, the entire island was in American hands.

After Tarawa, the 8th Marines sailed for the Hawaiian Islands. After a stop at Pearl Harbor, where the wounded were transferred to hospitals, the regiment traveled to the island of Hawaii and helped set up a base named Camp Tarawa. There, the Marines would rest, re-equip themselves, and prepare for their next landing: Saipan.

Now commanded by Colonel Clarence R. Wallace, a veteran of the battle for Kwajalein, the 8th Marines furnished two battalions—the 2d and 3d—for the initial Saipan landing, on the morning of 15 June 1944. The assault waves were met by withering enemy fire and sustained heavy losses, but managed to move forward against Japanese strongholds after reaching the beach. The 1st Battalion, 8th Marines, soon joined the rest of the regiment ashore and helped expand its perimeter. Over the ensuing three weeks, the 8th Marines,

with other units of the 2d Marine Division, pushed northward, hampered equally by a tenacious foe and by the rugged, mountainous terrain of the island. Organized Japanese resistance finally ended on 9 July, although mopping-up operations would go on for some time after that.

With Saipan secure, the regiment was ordered to prepare for a landing on nearby Tinian. At dawn on 24 July, the 8th and 2d Marines conducted a feint off the beach at Tinian Town on the southwest coast. This diverted Japanese attention from the main landings by the 24th and 25th Marines of the 4th Marine Division, on two small beaches on the northern tip of the island. The 8th Marines came ashore the following morning and began moving north toward its objective, Ushi Point. Despite rocky terrain, thick undergrowth, a fierce two-day typhoon, and groups of the determined Japanese holed up in craggy coral outcroppings, the island was officially secured by 1 August. The 8th Marines then assumed sole responsibility for patrolling and mop-up activities, which lasted for months.

On 1 April 1945, the 8th Marines formed part of a division-sized feint against the southeast coast of Okinawa, while the main landings were taking place on the western coast. Shortly afterward, the regiment redeployed to Saipan, but before long was called back to Okinawan waters to seize offshore islands. It captured Iheya Shima on 3 June, then Aguni Shima on 9 June. In a final thrust against entrenched Japanese forces, the 8th Marines was called in to relieve the battle-worn 7th Marines on 18 June. That same day, U.S. Tenth Army commander Lieutenant General Simon B. Buckner was mortally wounded by enemy shelling while he was observing the battle progress in the 3d Battalion, 8th Marines' sector.

Marine Lieutenant General Roy S. Geiger, who had taken command of the Tenth Army after General Buckner's death, declared the island secured on 22 June 1945. The 8th Marines stayed on Okinawa until 1 July for mopping-up operations. The regiment then redeployed to Saipan where it rejoined the 2d Division, then in training for the projected invasion of Japan.

After the war ended in August 1945, the 8th Marines prepared to move to the island of Kyushu, where it would be assigned occupation duty. The regiment arrived at the devastated city of Nagasaki in late September. For the next nine months, it served alongside other 2d Marine Division and Army units of the occupation force. In June 1946, the 8th Marines received orders to return to the United States, to end four and a half years in the Pacific theater. After debarking in Norfolk, the regiment proceeded to Camp Lejeune, North Carolina, where the 2d Marine Division had established its new home.

The 8th Marines, after being reduced to the size of an infantry battalion, participated in Atlantic Fleet maneuvers in February 1948, then departed for the Mediterranean Sea, part of a second Marine amphibious unit which deployed with the Sixth Fleet. The deployment of such amphibious forces to the Mediterranean has since become routine and continuous, providing a base for rapid contingency response in the region. After another deployment to the Mediterranean in 1949, the 8th Marines was deactivated on 17 October 1949, a result of the ongoing postwar reorganization of a shrinking Marine Corps.

The outbreak of the Korean War, in June 1950, brought about reactivation of the 8th Marines by 9 August of that year. In June 1951, battalions of the regiment resumed their Mediterranean deployments, where they took part in North Atlantic Treaty Organization (NATO) exercises. In the Caribbean, other battalions—and on occasion the entire regiment—deployed frequently for training exercises.

A civil war in Lebanon during the summer of

Department of Defense Photo (USMC) A450302
A rifle squad from Company D, 1st Battalion, 8th Marines, attempts to locate a sniper firing at a position near the international safety zone in Santo Domingo, Dominican Republic, in May 1965.

1958 resulted in the landing of two battalions of the 8th Marines at Beirut during 18-21 July, as part of a larger peacekeeping force. The 1st Battalion, 8th Marines, which had deployed to the Mediterranean earlier in the year, came ashore in landing craft. The 2d Battalion, along with Company K of the 3d Battalion, arrived by airlift increments at Beirut International Airport. After calm was restored, the two battalions left Lebanon in September, returning to Camp Lejeune.

In the fall of 1962, the 8th Marines played a role in the Cuban missile crisis. As President John F. Kennedy, on 22 October, spoke to the American people about the presence of Soviet missiles in Cuba, the regiment, now commanded by Colonel Anthony Caputo, dispatched the 1st Battalion to reinforce the U.S. Naval Base at Guantanamo. The rest of the regiment's battalions went on board ship several days later to help establish a naval quarantine near Cuban waters. After the crisis eased, the 8th Marines redeployed to Camp Lejeune in increments during late November and early December.

On 26 October 1964, in a division-sized landing exercise codenamed Steel Pike 1, Colonel Richard S. Johnson's 8th Marines became the first regiment in the history of the Marine Corps to make an amphibious landing entirely by helicopter. The exercise was conducted off the coast of Spain.

In the spring of 1965, the 1st Battalion, 8th Marines, was airlifted to the Dominican Republic, joining two other 2d Division battalions that had been deployed as part of a joint task force to deal with worsening unrest there. For one month,

Department of Defense Photo (USN) DN-ST-84-01273

Personnel from Battalion Landing Team 1/8, 24th Marine Amphibious Unit, come ashore in late May 1983 at Beirut, Lebanon, debarking from a utility landing craft, ready to participate as part of the United Nations multinational peacekeeping force.

Marines of the battalion braved sniper fire to patrol its sector of the capital city of Santo Domingo. The 1st Battalion sailed back to Camp Lejeune on 3 June 1965.

Two non-routine deployments of the 1st and 3d Battalions, 8th Marines, occurred in 1970 and 1971, to New England and Washington, D.C., in connection with potential civil disturbances.

The regiment turned its attention to NATO's northern flank in a series of exercises beginning in the fall of 1976, before becoming the Marine Corps' dedicated Mediterranean regiment, tasked with providing battalions for routine deployment with the Sixth Fleet.

In May 1980, the 1st Battalion, 8th Marines, deployed to Key West, Florida, on a humanitarian mission, assigned to assist in receiving civilian refugees from Cuba and Haiti.

As the ground combat element of the 32d Marine Amphibious Unit (MAU), Battalion Landing Team 2/8 assisted in the evacuation of American citizens from Lebanon in late June 1982. It then landed at Beirut in August as part of a multinational peacekeeping force to oversee the two-week-long evacuation of Palestinian guerrillas. Re-embarking shortly after the guerrillas left, the Marines were ordered back to Beirut in late September. They established positions near the Beirut International Airport. Over the next 18 months, all three battalions of the 8th Marines were rotated through Beirut, as the ground components of the 24th and 22d MAUs, serving as part

Infantrymen from Company F, 2d Battalion, 8th Marines, begin patrolling on the island of Carriacou after a pre-dawn, surprise landing on 1 November 1983. The landing on Carriacou took place seven days after the initial American assault on nearby Grenada.

of the multinational peacekeeping force.

At 0622 on Sunday morning, 23 October 1983, a suicide truck-bomb attack on the headquarters building of the 1st Battalion at the Beirut International Airport resulted in 220 Marine deaths, the largest loss of Marines on a single day since World War II. Meanwhile in the Caribbean, Battalion Landing Team 2/8, part of the 22d MAU enroute to Lebanon, was diverted to Grenada for operations in conjunction with other American and Caribbean forces. At 0500 on 25 October, Marines conducted

a helicopterborne assault from the USS *Guam* (LPH-9) on Pearls Airport. By 2 November, the Marines had concluded operations on Grenada, secured the neighboring island of Carriacou, and were back on their way to Lebanon, where they remained until February 1984.

The regiment's traditional high level of operational readiness was tested again, in August 1990, when Iraqi forces invaded Kuwait. Accordingly, President George H. Bush ordered a major deployment of U.S. Armed Forces to the Persian Gulf to

Department of Defense Photo (USMC) 960705-M-39830-002

A Marine from Company K, 3d Battalion, 8th Marines, stands his post at the southern end of the U.S. Embassy grounds in Monrovia, Liberia, in August 1996.

prevent a possible Iraqi invasion of Saudi Arabia. The 2d Marine Division, including the 8th Marines, immediately intensified its training program in preparation for deployment to the Gulf.

On 12 December, the main body of the division began deployment to Saudi Arabia to take its place as part of I Marine Expeditionary Force (I MEF). As the 8th Marines had to leave two of its four battalions behind to cover any other MEF commitments which might arise, the 3d Battalion, 23d Marines, a Reserve unit headquartered in New Orleans, Louisiana, became the 8th Marines' third battalion. The 2d Battalion, 4th Marines, operationally attached to the regiment since mid-October, deployed to the Persian Gulf with the 8th Marines.

In Saudi Arabia, the regiment underwent extensive training in preparation for the expected assault into Kuwait. The initial weeks prior to the assault was a period of continuous activity for the regiment, as it prepared to move to its final assembly areas. The 8th Marines also acquired an extra armored "punch" during this period, as two companies of the 4th Tank Battalion were assigned to the regiment.

In the early morning hours of 24 February 1991, the 8th Marines advanced through breaches in the Iraqi minefields and attacked enemy positions inside of Kuwait. Units of the regiment were responsible for the destruction of dozens of enemy tanks and vehicles, hundreds of Iraqi casualties, and more than 1,200 enemy prisoners of war. As the 8th Marines continued to clear its sector of enemy forces, a 28 February ceasefire ended the fighting with a complete Coalition victory.

In March, while the 2d Marine Division command post displaced to Saudi Arabia, the 8th Marines remained in Kuwait under the operational control of Marine Forces Southwest Asia, in order

Photo courtesy of Maj Nathan S. Lowrey, USMCR

Marines from Weapons Company, Battalion Landing Team 3/8, in Gnjilane, Kosovo, in July 1999, during Operation Joint Guardian.

to provide a "presence" of U.S. forces in the area. Elements of the regiment participated from April to July 1991 in Operation Provide Comfort, which was designed to provide humanitarian assistance to the Kurdish populations of northern Iraq. The bulk of the regiment remained in Kuwait until early May, when it was ordered to return to Al Jubayl in Saudi Arabia. At that time, the regiment returned to the operational control of the 2d Marine Division, and began preparation for deployment back to Camp Lejeune. The 8th Marines was the last Marine ground combat unit to leave Kuwait. The long-awaited deployment home was completed in mid-May, when the Marines received a well-deserved welcome at Camp Lejeune.

The remainder of the decade proved eventful for the 8th Marines. The regiment's operational skill and readiness was thoroughly tested, as elements of the 8th Marines participated in military operations and humanitarian missions in support of American foreign policy interests. During the 1990s Marines from the regiment were deployed to Bosnia (1993 and 1994), Cuba and the Caribbean area (1993 and 1994), the Central African Republic (1996), and Liberia (1996), where their presence supported a variety of missions, including non-combatant evacuations, humanitarian relief operations, and the restoration of order and democracy. During the last years of the decade, elements of the regiment participated in the enforcement of United Nations resolutions in Albania and in Kosovo, as the spread of ethnic conflict in the former Yugoslavia threatened the stability of Eastern Europe.

8th Marines
Commanding Officers

Maj Ellis B. Miller . . . . 11 October 1917 - 12 October 1917
LtCol George C. Reid . . . . 13 October 1917 - 24 October 1917
Maj Ellis B. Miller . . . . 25 October 1917 - 2 November 1917
Col Laurence H. Moses . . . . 3 November 1917 - 8 March 1919
LtCol Theodore E. Backstrom . . . . 9 March 1919 - 10 April 1919

LtCol Louis McC. Little . . . . 5 January 1920 - 30 April 1921
Col Dickinson P. Hall . . . . 1 May 1921 - 31 October 1921
LtCol Harry R. Hall . . . . 1 November 1921 - 7 April 1923
Col James T. Bootes . . . . 8 April 1923 - 29 April 1923
LtCol Harry R. Lay . . . . 30 April 1923 - 30 May 1923

Col James T. Bootes . . . . 31 May 1923 - 20 July 1924
LtCol William L. Redles . . . . 21 July 1924 - 23 July 1924
Col Harold C. Snyder . . . . 24 July 1924 - 1 July 1925
Col Leo D. Hermle . . . . 1 April 1940 - 23 July 1940
Col Henry L. Larsen . . . . 24 July 1940 - 31 October 1941

LtCol Victor F. Bleasdale . . . . 1 November 1941 - 11 December 1941
Col Henry L. Larsen . . . . 12 December 1941 - 22 December 1941
LtCol Richard H. Jeschke . . . . 23 December 1941 - 3 May 1943
Col Elmer E. Hall . . . . 4 May 1943 - 14 December 1943
LtCol Paul D. Sherman . . . . 15 December 1943 - 1 January 1944

LtCol John H. Griebel . . . . 2 January 1944 - 9 April 1944
Col Clarence R. Wallace . . . . 10 April 1944 - 28 June 1945
Col James F. Shaw . . . . 29 June 1945 - 14 July 1945
Col Thomas G. McFarland . . . . 15 July 1945 - 1 April 1947
Col Reginald H. Ridgely . . . . 2 April 1947 - 28 September 1948

LtCol Richard C. Nutting . . . . 29 September 1948 - 31 October 1948
LtCol Arthur N.B. Robertson . . . . 1 November 1948 - 16 October 1949
Maj Anthony Walker . . . . 10 August 1950 - 5 September 1950
LtCol Norman E. Sparling . . . . 6 September 1950 - 21 September 1950
Col James M. Masters, Jr. . . . . 22 September 1950 - 16 March 1952

Col John H. Masters . . . . 17 March 1952 - 1 February 1953
Col Dewolf Schatzel . . . . 2 February 1953 - 13 May 1954
Col Alexander A. Vandegrift, Jr. . . . . 14 May 1954 - 6 February 1955
Col Marlowe C. Williams . . . . 7 February 1955 - 12 December 1955
Col Glen C. Funk . . . . 13 December 1955 - 4 May 1956

Col Kenyth A. Damke . . . . 5 May 1956 - 29 August 1956
Col Thomas J. Colley . . . . 30 August 1956 - 31 August 1957
Col Robert C. Burns . . . . 1 September 1957 - 28 July 1958
Col George W. Killen . . . . 29 July 1958 - 2 July 1959
Col Ronald A. Van Stockum . . . . 3 July 1959 - 10 June 1960

Col Victor R. Bisceglia . . . . 11 June 1960 - 17 March 1961
Col Ronald E. Carey . . . . 18 March 1961 - 6 March 1962
Col Anthony Caputo . . . . 7 March 1962 - 1 June 1963
Col James O. Bell . . . . 2 June 1963 - 1 June 1964
Col Richard S. Johnson . . . . 2 June 1964 - 28 June 1965

Col Gerald F. Russell . . . . 29 June 1965 - 15 July 1966
Col George D. Webster . . . . 16 July 1966 - 28 December 1966
LtCol Curtis A. James, Jr. . . . . 28 December 1966 - 9 January 1967
Col William H. Mulvey . . . . 10 January 1967 - 9 October 1968
Col William M. Van Zuyen . . . . 10 October 1968 - 19 March 1969

LtCol John R. Greenstone . . . . 20 March 1969 - 6 February 1970
Col Harold A. Hatch . . . . 7 February 1970 - 19 June 1970
LtCol Charles M.C. Jones, Jr. . . . . 20 June 1970 - 17 September 1970
Col Lemuel C. Shepherd III . . . . 18 September 1970 - 8 June 1971
Col Edwin M. Young . . . . 9 June 1971 - 2 June 1972

LtCol Oswald P. Paredes . . . . 3 June 1972 - 6 September 1972
Col Stanley Davis . . . . 7 September 1972 - 27 June 1973
LtCol Daniel C. Daly . . . . 28 June 1973 - 13 July 1973
Col William D. Kent . . . . 14 July 1973 - 24 July 1974
Col Gerald C. Thomas, Jr. . . . . 25 July 1974 - 21 August 1975

Col Alexander P. McMillan . . . . 22 August 1975 - 27 January 1977
Col Americo A. Sardo . . . . 28 January 1977 - 21 March 1978
Col William R. Ball . . . . 22 March 1978 - 5 June 1979
Col Michael K. Sheridan . . . . 6 June 1979 - 5 June 1980
Col Jim R. Joy . . . . 6 June 1980 - 9 August 1981

Col Laurence R. Gaboury . . . . 10 August 1981 - 7 February 1983
Col Robert B. Johnston . . . . 8 February 1983 - 22 May 1984
Col John P. Brickley . . . . 23 May 1984 - 13 November 1986
Col John J. Sheehan . . . . 14 November 1986 - 16 May 1988
LtCol Ray L. Smith . . . . 17 May 1988 - 19 June 1990

Col Larry S. Schmidt . . . . 20 June 1990 - 5 June 1992
Col Keith T. Holcomb . . . . 6 June 1992 - 1 December 1993
Col Jennings B. Beavers . . . . 2 December 1993 - 26 July 1995
Col Tony L. Corwin . . . . 27 July 1995 - 27 June 1997
Col Joseph J. Streitz . . . . 28 June 1997 - 31 July 1998

Col James W. Davis . . . . 1 August 1998 - 10 July 2000
Col Mastin M. Robeson . . . . 11 July 2000 -

8th Marines
LINEAGE

1917 - 1919

ACTIVATED 9 OCTOBER 1917 AT QUANTICO, VIRGINIA, AS THE 8TH REGIMENT

RELOCATED DURING NOVEMBER 1917 TO FORT CROCKETT, TEXAS

ASSIGNED DURING AUGUST 1918 TO THE 3D PROVISIONAL BRIGADE

RELOCATED DURING APRIL 1919 TO PHILADELPHIA, PENNSYLVANIA

DEACTIVATED 25 APRIL 1919

1920 - 1925

REACTIVATED 5 JANUARY 1920 AT PORT-AU-PRINCE, HAITI, AND ASSIGNED
TO THE 1ST PROVISIONAL BRIGADE

PARTICIPATED IN OPERATIONS AGAINST DISSIDENTS, JANUARY 1920 - JUNE 1925

DEACTIVATED 1 JULY 1925

1940 - 1949

REACTIVATED 1 APRIL 1940 AT SAN DIEGO, CALIFORNIA, AS THE 8TH MARINES,
2D MARINE BRIGADE

2D MARINE BRIGADE REDESIGNATED 1 FEBRUARY 1941 AS 2D MARINE DIVISION,
FLEET MARINE FORCE

ASSIGNED DURING DECEMBER 1941 TO 2D MARINE BRIGADE, 2D MARINE DIVISION

DEPLOYED DURING OCTOBER 1942 TO AMERICAN SAMOA AND DETACHED FROM
THE 2D MARINE DIVISION

DETACHED DURING OCTOBER 1942 FROM THE 2D MARINE BRIGADE

ASSIGNED DURING FEBRUARY 1943 TO THE 2D MARINE DIVISION

PARTICIPATED IN THE FOLLOWING WORLD WAR II CAMPAIGNS

GUADALCANAL
TARAWA
SAIPAN
TINIAN
OKINAWA

DEPLOYED DURING SEPTEMBER-OCTOBER 1945 TO NAGASAKI, JAPAN

PARTICIPATED IN THE OCCUPATION OF JAPAN, OCTOBER 1945 - JUNE 1946

RELOCATED DURING JUNE-JULY 1946 TO CAMP LEJEUNE, NORTH CAROLINA

ASSIGNED DURING NOVEMBER 1948 TO THE 2D PROVISIONAL MARINE REGIMENT

DEACTIVATED 17 OCTOBER 1949

1950 - 1990

REACTIVATED 9 AUGUST 1950 AT CAMP LEJEUNE, NORTH CAROLINA, AND
ASSIGNED TO THE 2D MARINE DIVISION

ELEMENTS PARTICIPATED IN THE LANDINGS IN LEBANON,
JULY-SEPTEMBER 1958

PARTICIPATED IN THE CUBAN MISSILE CRISIS, OCTOBER-DECEMBER 1962

ELEMENTS PARTICIPATED IN THE INTERVENTION IN THE DOMINICAN REPUBLIC, MAY-JUNE 1965

PARTICIPATED IN NUMEROUS TRAINING EXERCISES THROUGHOUT THE 1970S

ELEMENTS PARTICIPATED AS PART OF THE MULTINATIONAL PEACEKEEPING FORCE IN LEBANON,
AUGUST 1982 - FEBRUARY 1984

ELEMENTS PARTICIPATED IN THE LANDINGS ON GRENADA - CARRIACOU,
OCTOBER-NOVEMBER 1983

1990 - 1999

ELEMENT PARTICIPATED IN OPERATION SHARP EDGE, LIBERIA,
AUGUST 1990 - JANUARY 1991

PARTICIPATED IN OPERATIONS DESERT SHIELD AND DESERT STORM, SOUTHWEST ASIA,
DECEMBER 1990 - APRIL 1991

ELEMENTS PARTICIPATED IN OPERATION PROVIDE COMFORT, IRAQ,
APRIL-JULY 1991

ELEMENTS PARTICIPATED IN SUPPORT OF OPERATIONS PROVIDE PROMISE AND DENY FLIGHT,
BOSNIA, SEPTEMBER-OCTOBER 1993 AND JANUARY 1994

ELEMENTS PARTICIPATED IN SUPPORT OF OPERATION SUPPORT DEMOCRACY, CUBA AND
CARIBBEAN AREA, OCTOBER-NOVEMBER 1993 AND MAY-JULY 1994

ELEMENT PARTICIPATED IN SUPPORT OF OPERATION SEA SIGNAL, CUBA,
JUNE-JULY 1994

ELEMENT PARTICIPATED IN OPERATION QUICK RESPONSE, CENTRAL AFRICAN REPUBLIC,
MAY 1996

ELEMENT PARTICIPATED IN OPERATION ASSURED RESPONSE, LIBERIA,
APRIL-AUGUST 1996

ELEMENTS PARTICIPATED IN OPERATIONS IN ALBANIA, MARCH-MAY 1997 AND
APRIL-MAY 1999

ELEMENT PARTICIPATED IN OPERATIONS IN KOSOVO,
JUNE-JULY 1999

8th Marines
HONORS

PRESIDENTIAL UNIT CITATION STREAMER WITH TWO BRONZE STARS

WORLD WAR II
GUADALCANAL - 1942
TARAWA - 1943
OKINAWA - 1945

NAVY UNIT COMMENDATION STREAMER

SOUTHWEST ASIA
1990 - 1991

WORLD WAR I VICTORY STREAMER

HAITIAN CAMPAIGN STREAMER

MARINE CORPS EXPEDITIONARY STREAMER WITH TWO BRONZE STARS

AMERICAN DEFENSE SERVICE STREAMER

ASIATIC-PACIFIC CAMPAIGN STREAMER WITH ONE SILVER STAR

WORLD WAR II VICTORY STREAMER

NAVY OCCUPATION SERVICE STREAMER WITH "ASIA" AND "EUROPE"

NATIONAL DEFENSE SERVICE STREAMER WITH TWO BRONZE STARS

ARMED FORCES EXPEDITIONARY STREAMER WITH FOUR BRONZE STARS

SOUTHWEST ASIA SERVICE STREAMER WITH THREE BRONZE STARS

The 10th Marines

The 10th Regiment was activated at Quantico, Virginia, on 15 January 1918, under the command of Major Robert H. Dunlap. It was organized from units of the Mobile Artillery Force, an outgrowth of the artillery battalion formed at Veracruz, Mexico, in 1914 and later deployed to Haiti and Santo Domingo. The 10th Regiment was formed to support the Marine regiments of the American Expeditionary Force in France. Plans called for a Marine artillery regiment to man 7-inch naval guns in support of an all-Marine division during the extensive Allied operations planned for 1919. The signing of the Armistice found the unit still training in the United States. Postwar demobilization soon brought a marked drawdown on the regiment's strength.

Reorganized several times during the 1920s, the 10th Regiment supplied personnel for expeditions to the Caribbean and the Pacific. During the early 1920s, the regiment took part in annual recreations of famous Civil War battles: The Wilderness in 1921, Gettysburg in 1922, New Market in 1923, and Antietam in 1924. Elements of the 10th Regiment also went to Culebra, Puerto Rico, and the territory of Hawaii. On 14 November 1924, all companies were renamed as batteries. During October 1926, the 10th Regiment (less the 4th Battery, 2d Battalion) was assigned to guard the U.S. mails, in

Marines man a 3-inch field piece in full recoil, used in the Dominican Republic in 1916.
Department of Defense Photo (USMC) A521542

Elements of the 10th Marines, along with members of several other Marine Corps units, were assigned the task of guarding mail in the wake of a series of robberies in the 1920s.

the wake of a series of robberies. In four months of guard duty in the Midwest, no shots were fired by Marines and no Marine-guarded mail was lost. In February of the following year, the unit returned

A battalion of the 10th Marines is inspected in Tientsin, China in 1928. From left are Col Harry Lay, USMC; MajGen Joseph C. Castner, USA, the commander of U.S. Forces in China; BGen Smedley D. Butler, USMC; and LtCol Ellis B. Miller, USMC.

Department of Defense Photo (USMC) A515290

to Quantico, where it was placed on a stand-by basis for expeditionary service in China.

Elements of the 10th Regiment deployed to Tientsin, China, during June 1927. As part of the 3d Brigade, under the command of Brigadier General Smedley D. Butler, the unit provided security for American lives and property until October 1928, when it returned to Quantico.

On 10 July 1930, reflecting a Corps-wide change of "Regiment" to "Marines," the 10th Regiment was redesignated the 10th Marines. After the formation of the Fleet Marine Force in 1933, the 10th Marines took part in fleet landing and training exercises from Hawaii to Puerto Rico through the rest of the decade. During this period the 2d Battalion, 10th Marines, was activated at San Diego.

During late spring of 1941, artillery batteries of the 2d Battalion, 10th Marines, were attached to the 6th Marines, for deployment to Iceland. The artillerymen returned to the United States and rejoined the 10th Marines on 1 April 1942.

At the outbreak of World War II, the 10th Marines was attached to the 2d Marine Division and stationed at Camp Elliott, San Diego, California.

Department of Defense Photo (USMC) A524206

A group of British Army and U.S. Marine officers observe the operations of a 75mm howitzer gun crew in maneuvers in Iceland, 1941-1942.

Elements of the regiment began deploying in early 1942: first to American Samoa, later to New Zealand.

In August 1942, the 3d Battalion, 10th Marines, attached to the 2d Marines, 1st Marine Division, was among the first units to land at Guadalcanal. Following the initial landing, the 3d Battalion, 10th Marines, landed on Tulagi during early August, with remaining elements of the regiment arriving in October. The 1st and 3d Battalions provided artillery support during the heavy fighting on Guadalcanal, and the 1st and 2d Battalions took part in the final drive against the enemy. After the Guadalcanal campaign, the 10th Marines went through a period of rehabilitation, reorganization, and training at Wellington, New Zealand.

During the period, while the regiment prepared for the Tarawa landing, Colonel Thomas E. Bourke was promoted to brigadier general—becoming the first "commanding general" of the 10th Marines—and the regiment absorbed a fifth battalion. After remaining at sea as regimental reserve during the initial assault on Betio Island, the 10th Marines delivered direct fire in support of the 2d and 8th Marines on 21 November 1943. By that afternoon, the entire 1st Battalion, 10th Marines, had come ashore. The following morning, batteries of the 2d Battalion, 10th Marines, landed on the neighboring island of Bairiki, subsequently directing heavy fire

on Betio. On the morning of 23 November, the 4th Battalion, 10th Marines, landed on Betio to support the final attack. During this attack, however, the infantry advance was so quick and the fighting took place at such close quarters that fire missions became infeasible. The entire island was in American hands by the end of the day.

In December 1943, following relocation to Hawaii and passage of command to Colonel Raphael Griffin, preparations began for the Saipan operation. On the afternoon of D-Day, 15 June 1944, the 1st and 2d Battalions, 10th Marines, landed on the west coast of the island, to support infantry and tank units that had landed earlier in the day and sustained heavy casualties. These battalions helped drive back the Japanese during a counterattack in the early morning hours of the 16th. Later that afternoon, the 3d and 4th Battalions landed. The damage suffered from the direct Japanese fire on the regimental command post and fire direction center on the night of 23-24 June forced the 1st Battalion, 10th Marines, to temporarily assume regimental fire control responsibilities. Supported by heavy artillery fire, units of the 2d and 4th Marine Division, along with the U.S. Army's 27th Division, continued to push the Japanese off the island. The 3d and 4th Battalions, 10th Marines, were attached to the 4th Marine Division to reinforce the 14th Marines and successfully helped repulse thousands of enemy soldiers in a desperate banzai attack on the morning of 7 July. The Marines fired their howitzers at point blank range before seizing pistols, rifles, and automatic rifles, to fight as infantry. The 3d Battalion, 10th Marines, was later awarded the Navy Unit Commendation by Secretary of the Navy James Forrestal.

After Saipan was declared secure on 9 July, the 10th Marines turned its attention toward operations on nearby Tinian. The campaign to capture Tinian began with the steady and methodical bombardment of the island from the southern end of Saipan from 9-23 July 1944. On the morning of 24 July, while the 2d and 8th Marines conducted a successful diversionary feint off the beach at Tinian Town, elements of the 4th Marine Division found light resistance at the actual landing sites. During the landings which followed, battalions of the 10th Marines were assigned to the 4th Marine Division initially. Later they went back to the 2d Marine Division. On 27 July, the 3d and 4th Battalions, 10th Marines, joined other 10th Marine units. For the remainder of the battle, all battalions of the 10th Marines fired in direct support of the 2d, 6th, and 8th Marines. After the island was secured, the 10th Marines returned to Saipan for rest and training.

On 27 March 1945, the 2d Marine Division embarked at Saipan and sailed 1,200 miles westward to Okinawa. On 1 April, while Marine and Army units landed on the west coast of the island, the 2d Marine Division conducted a demonstration on the southeast coast to confuse the Japanese defenders. For the first part of April, the 10th Marines formed part of the floating reserve off the southern coast of Okinawa, until a growing threat of Kamikaze attacks on U.S. ships caused the 2d

The pack howitzer is shown firing into a cave of Japanese soldiers from the brink of a cliff on Tinian on 25 August 1944. The artillery piece was lashed securely in its unusual position after being carried in parts by weary Marines to the edge of the embankment.

Department of Defense Photo (USMC) A94660

Department of Defense Photo (USMC) A15983

Marine artillery firing during training operations on Vieques Island, Puerto Rico, in March 1954.

Marine Division to return to Saipan. The 2d Battalion, 10th Marines, returned to Okinawa in June as part of a landing force that had been tasked with seizing several offshore islands. Later that month, the 2d Battalion served as supporting artillery for the 8th Marines and assisted in the final assault on the southern end of the island. The 10th Marines then returned to Saipan and its surrounding islands for artillery and maneuver exercises, remaining there until the end of the war.

During late September 1945, the 10th Marines relocated to Nagasaki, on the island of Kyushu, to assist in the occupation of Japan. The 2d Division remained in Japan, and eventually became solely responsible for the occupation of the island of Kyushu. The 10th Marines was one of the last units to leave Japan, after being relieved by the U. S. Army's 24th Division during June 1946. It reached its new home, at Camp Lejeune, North Carolina, in July.

Despite reduced strength as a result of postwar demobilization, elements of the 10th Marines participated in a great variety of training exercises, deployments, and field artillery demonstrations, including some at the familiar prewar training site of Culebra, Puerto Rico. A major reorganization during November 1947 resulted in the deactivation of all four artillery battalions, which were replaced by batteries. Following several additional reorganizations, the 10th Marines units were redesignated as 11th Marines units, in an effort to build up the 1st Marine Division artillery for deployment to Korea during the summer of 1950. Meanwhile, a new regiment, built primarily on Marine reservists, was formed at Camp Lejeune.

Throughout the 1950s, training of the expanding 10th Marines intensified. Much of the time, the 10th Marines took part in maneuvers in the Caribbean and on the East Coast of the United States. At times, elements of the 10th Marines par-

Department of Defense Photo (USMC) A452660

A gun crew from Battery L, 3d Battalion, 10th Marines, prepares to load a 155mm howitzer (towed) while conducting a live fire exercise at Camp Lejeune, North Carolina, during the 1970s. Below, Marines from the 4th Battalion, 10th Marines, participate in a civil disturbance training exercise at Camp Lejeune in October 1972.

Department of Defense Photo (USMC) A451693

ticipated in North Atlantic Treaty Organization operations in the North Sea and the Mediterranean.

During July 1958, rising tensions in the Middle East resulted in three battalion landing teams, with accompanying batteries from the 10th Marines landing at Beirut. The Marines stayed in Lebanon until October.

In late October 1962, the 10th Marines deployed with the 2d Marine Division during the Cuban missile crisis. The regiment's units remained on board amphibious shipping until December.

The 2d and 3d Battalions, 10th Marines, were among the units sent to the Dominican Republic during April 1965, to support Marine infantry battalions assigned to restore order to the city of Santo Domingo during political upheavals. These artillery units were set up in the vicinity of the Embajadore Hotel where American citizens were being assembled for evacuation. All elements of the 10th Marines had left the Dominican Republic by late May.

Department of Defense Photo (USMC) DM-ST-91-11583

Marine artillerymen fire their M-198 155mm howitzer in support of the opening of the ground offensive to free Kuwait during Operation Desert Storm in February 1991.

During the war in Vietnam, the understrength 2d Marine Division continued to meet its Mediterranean and Caribbean commitments, which required artillery batteries to deploy with battalion landing teams.

Throughout the 1970s and 1980s, the 10th Marines continued to participate in a variety of training exercises, including several NATO exercises in northern Europe and semi-annual firing exercises at Fort Bragg, North Carolina. Beginning in the summer of 1982, artillery batteries of the 10th Marines were deployed to Beirut in support of the Marine amphibious unit (MAU) serving there with the multinational peacekeeping force. The regiment continued to provide artillery support over the next 18 months to the MAUs stationed in Beirut. In October 1983, a battery of the 10th Marines formed a provisional rifle company to take part in the successful operations against Communist forces on the island of Grenada.

The regiment's ability to respond quickly to a crisis was tested again, this time in August 1990, when the military forces of Iraq's Saddam Hussein

invaded and occupied Kuwait. President George H. Bush immediately ordered American forces, including Marines, to the Persian Gulf, to prevent a possible Iraqi invasion of Saudi Arabia.

Elements of the 10th Marines began departing Camp Lejeune on 11 December, enroute to Saudi Arabia and Operation Desert Shield. As several elements of the regiment remained either at Camp Lejeune or on Okinawa to support other commitments, the 10th Marines was augmented by batteries from the 12th Marines and 14th Marines, a Reserve unit. The mission of the 10th Marines during Operation Desert Shield was to provide effective artillery support to the 2d Marine Division, and upon arrival in Saudi Arabia, the regiment undertook an intensive training program.

On 17 January 1991, the military operation in Southwest Asia was renamed Operation Desert Storm with the onset of Allied offensive air operations against Iraq. The 10th Marines tactical posture soon changed from defensive to offensive, as training intensified for combat operations.

On 27 January 1991, the 10th Marines fired its

Department of Defense Photo (USMC) DSP-94-A00262

Personnel from 1st Battalion, 10th Marines, off load from a LCAC near the port of Cap Haitien, Haiti, during Operation Uphold Democracy in September 1994.

first artillery mission against Iraqi forces, when elements of the regiment conducted an artillery raid just east of the Al Wahfrah oil field in Kuwait. This was the first offensive action by the 10th Marines since World War II. Several days later, on 29 January, Iraqi forces commenced full-scale probing actions across the Saudi Arabian border with tanks and mechanized forces. Engagements were out of range of 10th Marines artillery positions, which precluded the regiment's participation in the actions.

On 24 February, the Coalition forces unleashed its major ground offensive to liberate Kuwait. Throughout the ensuing days of combat, the 10th Marines provided close and continuous fire in support of the 2d Marine Division. The regiment fired counter-battery missions with deadly effectiveness when enemy targets were acquired. In one of the most memorable artillery actions of the campaign, virtually an entire Iraqi self-propelled battalion was acquired on radar and eliminated by accurate artillery fire from the 10th Marines.

After the 28 February 1991 ceasefire which ended the fighting, the 10th Marines prepared to depart the Persian Gulf for home. A detachment from 3d Battalion, 10th Marines, remained in Kuwait, and would later participate in Operation Provide Comfort in Iraq, which was designed to provide disaster relief and establish security zones for Kurdish refugees. However, the bulk of the regiment redeployed during April to Camp Lejeune, and a much-deserved welcome home.

Throughout the remaining years of the decade, elements of the 10th Marines participated in Operation Safe Harbor in Guantanamo Bay, Cuba (1991), and in Operations Restore Democracy, Support Democracy, and Uphold Democracy in Haiti (1994). The first operation provided humanitarian assistance to Haitians fleeing their country's internal power struggles, while in the latter three operations, the regiment participated with other American forces in helping to restore democracy to the strife-torn nation of Haiti. Elements of the regiment also participated during 1994 in Operations Able Manner and Able Vigil in the Florida Straits, which supported U.S. Navy and Coast Guard efforts to interdict Haitian and Cuban migrants off the Straits of Florida.

10th Marines
Commanding Officers

Maj Robert H. Dunlap . . . . 25 April 1914 - 17 February 1918
Maj Chandler Campbell . . . . 18 February 1918 - 30 November 1918
Col Dion Williams . . . . 1 December 1918 - 3 March 1919
Maj Ralph L. Shepard . . . . 4 March 1919 - 20 April 1919
LtCol Richard M. Cutts . . . . 21 April 1919 - 8 January 1922

LtCol Chandler Campbell . . . . 9 January 1922 - 15 August 1923
Maj Robert O. Underwood . . . . 16 August 1923 - 31 May 1925
Maj Emile P. Moses . . . . 1 June 1925 - 28 August 1925
Maj Howard W. Stone . . . . 29 August 1925 - 13 September 1925
Col Harry R. Lay . . . . 14 September 1925 - 26 November 1928

Maj Alexander A. Vandegrift . . . . 27 November 1928 - 18 December 1928
Maj James L. Underhill . . . . 19 December 1928 - 13 November 1930
LtCol Andrew B. Drum . . . . 14 November 1930 - 9 July 1933
Maj Fred S. N. Erskine . . . . 10 July 1933 - 12 September 1933
LtCol Harold S. Fasset (1st Bn) . . . . 13 September 1933 - 29 July 1936

LtCol Thomas E. Bourke (1st Bn) . . . . 30 July 1936 - 5 September 1936
LtCol Lloyd L. Leech (2d Bn) . . . . 6 September 1936 - 24 May 1937
LtCol Thomas E. Bourke (1st Bn) . . . . 25 May 1937 - 2 May 1938
Maj William H. Harrison (2d Bn) . . . . 3 May 1938 - 5 June 1938
LtCol Raphael Griffin (1st Bn) . . . . 6 June 1938 - 3 June 1940

LtCol John B. Wilson (2d Bn) . . . . 4 June 1940 - 26 December 1940
Col Thomas E. Bourke . . . . 27 December 1940 - 5 August 1942
Col John B. Wilson . . . . 6 August 1942 - 31 August 1942
LtCol Ralph E. Forysth . . . . 1 September 1942 - 22 November 1942
BGen Thomas E. Bourke . . . . 23 November 1942 - 9 December 1943

Col Raphael Griffin . . . . 10 December 1943 - 30 November 1944
LtCol Saville T. Clark . . . . 1 December 1944 - 31 December 1944
Col Bert A. Bone . . . . 1 January 1945 - 9 June 1945
Col Saville T. Clark . . . . 10 June 1945 - 7 June 1947
Col Randall M. Victory . . . . 8 June 1947 - 11 November 1947

Col Robert B. Luckey . . . . 12 November 1947 - 15 June 1949
LtCol Thomas S. Ivey . . . . 16 June 1949 - 14 July 1949
Col Wilburt S. Brown . . . . 15 July 1949 - 3 April 1951
LtCol Claude S. Sanders, Jr. . . . . 4 April 1951 - 4 May 1951
Col Jack Tabor . . . . 5 May 1951 - 14 July 1952

Col Donald M. Weller . . . . 15 July 1952 - 5 June 1953
Col Joe C. McHaney . . . . 6 June 1953 - 5 June 1954
Col Louie C. Reinberg . . . . 6 June 1954 - 18 June 1955
Col Merritt Adelman . . . . 19 June 1955 - 1 August 1956
Col Ransom M. Wood . . . . 2 August 1956 - 9 June 1957

LtCol Robert H. Armstrong	10 June 1957 - 3 July 1957
Col George B. Thomas	4 July 1957 - 21 June 1958
Col Frederick J. Karch	22 June 1958 - 1 December 1959
Col Carl A. Youngdale	2 December 1959 - 14 February 1961
LtCol Edmund E. Allen	15 February 1961 - 29 March 1961
Col Wade H. Hitt	30 March 1961 - 1 September 1962
Col William P. Oliver, Jr.	2 September 1962 - 27 June 1963
Col Henry H. Reichner, Jr.	28 June 1963 - 6 March 1964
Col John R. Chaisson	7 March 1964 - 10 February 1965
Col Herman Poggemeyer, Jr.	11 February 1965 - 31 May 1966
LtCol Edward A. Bailey	1 June 1966 - 8 July 1966
Col Charles E. Walker	9 July 1966 - 1 July 1968
Col Thomas J. Holt	2 July 1968 - 8 April 1971
Col Charles A. Webster	9 April 1971 - 15 July 1971
Col Charles R. Burroughs	16 July 1971 - 13 April 1972
LtCol Thomas A. McPheeters	14 April 1972 - 9 August 1972
Col Calhoun J. Killeen	10 August 1972 - 12 July 1973
Col Robert L. Milbrad	13 July 1973 - 11 January 1974
Col David A. Clark	12 January 1974 - 20 December 1974
Col Richard P. Johnson	21 December 1974 - 30 April 1976
Col William H. Rice	1 May 1976 - 12 May 1977
Col Francis Andriliunas	13 May 1977 - 11 July 1978
Col Martin D. Julian	12 July 1978 - 10 July 1980
Col Thomas W. Haven	11 July 1980 - 8 September 1981
Col Albert J. McCarthy, Jr.	9 September 1981 - 26 April 1983
Col Larry R. Williams	27 April 1983 - 31 May 1984
Col Christopher Catoe	1 June 1984 - 5 February 1986
Col James B. Way	6 February 1986 - 14 September 1987
Col Gary A. Blair	15 September 1987 - 28 June 1988
Col Thomas W. Roberts	29 June 1988 - 16 June 1989
Col Ronald G. Richard	17 June 1989 - 16 August 1990
Col Leslie M. Palm	17 August 1990 - 1 May 1992
Col Edward Hanlon, Jr.	2 May 1992 - 7 July 1993
Col Philip E. Hughes	8 July 1993 - 2 June 1995
Col James L. Sachtleben	3 June 1995 - 18 June 1997
Col Robert L. Click	19 June 1997 - 7 July 1999
Col Henry T. Gobar	8 July 1999 -

10th Marines
LINEAGE

1914 - 1917

ACTIVATED 25 APRIL 1914 AT VERACRUZ, MEXICO, AS ARTILLERY BATTALION AND ASSIGNED TO THE 1ST BRIGADE

RELOCATED DURING NOVEMBER-DECEMBER 1914 TO MARINE BARRACKS, ANNAPOLIS, MARYLAND, AND DETACHED FROM THE 1ST MARINE BRIGADE

DEPLOYED DURING AUGUST 1915 TO PORT-AU-PRINCE, HAITI, AND ASSIGNED TO THE 1ST BRIGADE

REDEPLOYED DURING MAY 1916 TO SANTO DOMINGO, DOMINICAN REPUBLIC

RELOCATED DURING JUNE-JULY 1916 TO SANTIAGO, DOMINICAN REPUBLIC

RELOCATED DURING NOVEMBER 1916 TO SANTO DOMINGO, DOMINICAN REPUBLIC

REASSIGNED DURING JANUARY 1917 TO THE 2D BRIGADE

RELOCATED DURING APRIL-MAY 1917 TO QUANTICO, VIRGINIA, AND DETACHED FROM THE 2D BRIGADE

REDESIGNATED 15 MAY 1917 AS THE 1ST FIELD ARTILLERY BATTALION

REDESIGNATED 1 AUGUST 1917 AS THE MOBILE ARTILLERY FORCE

1918 - 1940

REDESIGNATED 15 JANUARY 1918 AS THE 10TH REGIMENT

REDESIGNATED 1 APRIL 1920 AS THE 1ST SEPARATE FIELD ARTILLERY BATTALION

REDESIGNATED 1 JANUARY 1921 AS THE 10TH REGIMENT

PARTICIPATED IN THE GUARDING OF THE U.S. MAILS, OCTOBER 1926 - FEBRUARY 1927

HEADQUARTERS BATTERY, 10TH REGIMENT, DEACTIVATED 24 MAY 1927

ELEMENTS DEPLOYED TO TIENTSIN, CHINA, JUNE 1927 - OCTOBER 1928

REDESIGNATED 10 JULY 1930 AS THE 10TH MARINES

ELEMENTS OF THE REGIMENT REMAINED ON ACTIVE DUTY, 1927 - 1940

1940 - 1957

REACTIVATED 27 DECEMBER 1940 AT SAN DIEGO, CALIFORNIA, AS THE
10TH MARINES AND ASSIGNED TO THE 2D MARINE BRIGADE

2D MARINE BRIGADE REDESIGNATED 1 FEBRUARY 1941 AS THE 2D MARINE DIVISION

ELEMENTS DEPLOYED TO ICELAND, JUNE 1941 - MARCH 1942

DEPLOYED DURING JANUARY-NOVEMBER 1942 TO THE SOUTH PACIFIC

PARTICIPATED IN THE FOLLOWING WORLD WAR II CAMPAIGNS

GUADALCANAL
SOUTHERN SOLOMONS
TARAWA
SAIPAN
TINIAN
OKINAWA

REDEPLOYED DURING SEPTEMBER 1945 TO NAGASAKI, JAPAN

PARTICIPATED IN THE OCCUPATION OF JAPAN, SEPTEMBER 1945 - JUNE 1946

RELOCATED DURING JUNE-JULY 1946 TO CAMP LEJEUNE, NORTH CAROLINA

1958 - 1989

ELEMENTS PARTICIPATED IN THE LANDINGS IN LEBANON, JULY-OCTOBER 1958

PARTICIPATED IN THE CUBAN MISSILE CRISIS, OCTOBER-NOVEMBER 1962

ELEMENTS PARTICIPATED IN THE INTERVENTION IN THE DOMINICAN REPUBLIC,
APRIL-JUNE 1965

PARTICIPATED IN NUMEROUS TRAINING EXERCISES THROUGHOUT THE 1970S

ELEMENTS PARTICIPATED AS PART OF THE MULTINATIONAL PEACEKEEPING FORCES IN LEBANON,
AUGUST 1982 - FEBRUARY 1984

ELEMENTS PARTICIPATED IN THE LANDINGS ON GRENADA, OCTOBER 1983

1990 - 1999

ELEMENTS PARTICIPATED IN OPERATION SHARP EDGE, LIBERIA, AUGUST 1990

PARTICIPATED IN OPERATIONS DESERT SHIELD AND DESERT STORM, SOUTHWEST ASIA,
AUGUST 1990 - APRIL 1991

ELEMENT PARTICIPATED IN OPERATION PROVIDE COMFORT, IRAQ, APRIL 1991

ELEMENT PARTICIPATED IN OPERATION SAFE HARBOR, GUANTANAMO BAY,
CUBA, NOVEMBER-DECEMBER 1991

ELEMENTS PARTICIPATED IN OPERATIONS RESTORE DEMOCRACY, SUPPORT DEMOCRACY,
AND UPHOLD DEMOCRACY, HAITI, JULY-OCTOBER 1994

ELEMENTS PARTICIPATED IN OPERATIONS ABLE MANNER AND ABLE VIGIL, FLORIDA STRAITS,
AUGUST-OCTOBER 1994

10th Marines
HONORS

PRESIDENTIAL UNIT CITATION STREAMER

WORLD WAR II
TARAWA - 1943

NAVY UNIT COMMENDATION STREAMER

SOUTHWEST ASIA
1990 - 1991

HAITIAN CAMPAIGN STREAMER

DOMINICAN CAMPAIGN STREAMER

WORLD WAR I VICTORY STREAMER WITH "WEST INDIES"

YANGTZE SERVICE STREAMER

MARINE CORPS EXPEDITIONARY STREAMER WITH TWO BRONZE STARS

AMERICAN DEFENSE SERVICE STREAMER

ASIATIC-PACIFIC CAMPAIGN STREAMER WITH ONE SILVER AND ONE BRONZE STAR

WORLD WAR II VICTORY STREAMER

NAVY OCCUPATION SERVICE STREAMER WITH "ASIA" AND "EUROPE"

NATIONAL DEFENSE SERVICE STREAMER WITH TWO BRONZE STARS

ARMED FORCES EXPEDITIONARY STREAMER

SOUTHWEST ASIA SERVICE STREAMER WITH THREE BRONZE STARS

The device reproduced on the back cover is the oldest military insignia in continuous use in the United States. It first appeared, as shown here, on Marine Corps buttons adopted in 1804. With the stars changed to five points, the device has continued on Marine Corps buttons to the present day.

Made in the USA
Columbia, SC
22 December 2024

50468055R00046